Love Activism

Love Activism

Stacy Russo

Litwin Books
Sacramento, CA

Copyright Stacy Russo, 2018
Published by Litwin Books, 2018

Litwin Books
PO Box 188784
Sacramento, CA 95818

http://litwinbooks.com

Printed on acid-free paper.

Library of Congress Cataloging-in-Publication Data

Names: Russo, Stacy Shotsberger, 1970- author.
Title: Love activism / Stacy Russo.
Description: Sacramento, CA : Litwin Books, 2018. | Includes bibliographical
  references and index.
Identifiers: LCCN 2018005615 | ISBN 9781634000550 (pbk. : alk. paper)
Subjects: LCSH: Love. | Social service. | Conduct of life.
Classification: LCC BF575.L8 R865 2018 | DDC 177/.7--dc23
LC record available at https://lccn.loc.gov/2018005615

Contents

About Love Activism

This book presents a new way to think of activism and the life of an activist. It is about working toward political and social change, as activism is often defined, but it is also about reimagining ideas and ways of activism. This is accomplished by valuing the profound nature of everyday activism and all of the components of the daily life of an activist, including even small actions and decisions. Love Activism is a form of activism that is not composed of isolated actions or single issues; it is a way of life. It is also not a light form of activism. The word "love" should not be equated with fluff, because love, if understood as an action and commitment, is deep and has far-reaching potential.

What, essentially, is Love Activism? The easiest definition is that Love Activism is a daily, radical, and holistic activism of kindness composed of eight elements: service, empathy, hope, non-violence, self-care, creativity, feminism, and mindfulness. The fruits it offers to the practitioner are infinite. It is a very present and powerful activism. Love Activism brings positive changes and rewards as types of everyday magic, since it is a wide-ranging activism we are able to infuse in all of our activities, whether they are small or large acts. It is a fully alive way to live against cruelty and violence. Love activists strive to live as much as possible outside of and in opposition to systems that promote violence and exploitation. Love Activism is concerned with all forms of oppression and blooms most beautifully when there is no bullying, meanness, sexism, racism, greed, ruthless competition, or any form of unjust discrimination. Throughout this book we will examine how to be a daily activist through personal stories, practical ideas, and discovering the lives of other activists. Love Activism is a practice that embraces Sarah Corbett's thoughts: "Activism should be threaded through all of our lives, in everything we do….when we vote, shop, travel, in all our interactions with people, and in all the decisions we make."[1] As we will see, opportunities for Love Activism are all around during the day and available to each of us.

Why is there a need for Love Activism? Those of us who are committed to living peaceful lives and actively working to bring harmony to the world may feel daunted when faced with such huge and well-funded opposition. Trying to dismantle large and cruel structures, such as systemic racism and a culture of violence against women, as well as inhumane corporations and institutions, can seem overwhelming, even if we are able to see some success and progressive change at times. Love Activism can help with this discouragement or potential burn-out by offering a way we can all make real and positive change in our daily lives. This is realized through how we perform our work, what we do in our communities, and how we go about our days mindfully and with kindness.

In Franciscan spirituality, there is a practice of seeing with the eye of our heart. I first heard about this way of seeing when listening to Murray Bodo's *The Way of St. Francis: Teachings and Practices for Daily Life.*[2] He comments that another way to describe this type of seeing is seeing with the eye of the soul. The world around us, Bodo explains, takes on a deeper dimension when we see in this manner. How we look at people and the landscape changes. We no longer live what he calls "one dimensional lives," but become "much more profound" people. We may be able to even do things we couldn't do before, because of a stillness and deeper way of living. We are calmer and more attentive. Looking at others and our world through this mindful, inner heart eye is the root of Love Activism.

The Scope and Shape of Love Activism

When we consider the scope of Love Activism, it is all-encompassing. Love Activism is an activism for ourselves, our communities, the world, and the earth. It is alive in caring deeply for our own needs, as much as it lives in what we do for others. In Love Activism, hierarchies do not exist and all life is

---

1 Sarah Corbett, *A Little Book of Craftivism* (London, England: Cicada Books, 2013), 60.

2 Murray Bodo, *The Way of St. Francis: Teachings and Practices for Daily Life*, Sounds True, 1999, compact disc.

understood as interconnected. It is present in everything we do, if we wish to fully embrace it.

If we imagined Love Activism as a shape, it would be a large, round, and colorful circle. One of the best explanations of this comes from *The Woman's Dictionary of Symbols and Sacred Objects*: "The universe begins with roundness...The great circle, the cosmic egg, the bubble, the spiral, the moon, the zero, the wheel of time, the infinite womb: such are the symbols that try to express a human sense of the wholeness of things."[3] If you can visualize this circle containing all of your favorite colors co-existing harmoniously, this is the world we imagine as love activists and how your life can feel when practicing daily, radical love.

Examining Our Lives

At the beginning of Thich Nhat Hanh's *At Home in the World: Stories and Essential Teachings from a Monk's Life*, he provides the following inscription: "Teaching is not done by talking alone. It is done by how you live your life. My life is my teaching. My life is my message."[4] This is much like the famous quote often attributed to Gandhi: "Be the change you wish to see in the world." How we live our lives can be the greatest example and inspiration for others. This leads to the need for self-examination.

As we practice Love Activism, we must honestly examine our lives, which may lead to making difficult changes or decisions, but will ultimately bring us lasting joy, peace, and balance. This occurs as we make changes that align with our ethical beliefs and take steps to remove inconsistencies that we may already be aware of, but struggle to act on. Our inability to act could stem from fear, convenience, or a pleasure we do not support, but have a hard time removing from our lives (examples of pleasures could be eating meat or buying products we like from a corporation we do not agree with). Or, it could be that we only focus on one cause and then do harm with other words or actions, such as a feminist who participates in racist speech or an animal rights activist who is sexist. As activists, we are committed to seeing the interconnections of all we do. This

---

3 Barbara G. Walker, *The Woman's Dictionary of Symbols and Sacred Objects* (San Francisco, CA: HarperCollins, 1995), 2.

4 Thich Nhat Hanh, *At Home in the World: Stories and Essential Teachings from a Monk's Life* (Berkeley, CA: Parallax Press, 2016), 5.

requires a willingness to continuously explore the intersections of all forms of oppression and realize when an action or in-action we are taking is putting us in the role of the oppressor.

While keeping this action of examining our lives in mind, it is important to also understand that Love Activism is not about perfection, because there is no such thing. We are human. No matter how much focus and good intention we have, we will fail at times to say the right thing and do what we know is the better way to act. We may make assumptions about people that reveal we have implicit biases within us, or we may find ourselves in a situation where we do not have the courage to speak up and suffer regret later. The important thing is that we realize our misstep and make an intention of trying to do better when faced with a similar incident in the future. We must never lose sight though that acknowledging where we fail is just the first step. The work we do or the actions we take to bring about change is when our acknowledgment becomes authentic.

A way to reflect on our authenticity and growth as activists is to consider the difference between learning and willful ignorance. Once I was telling a therapist about how tough I was on myself and how I felt "stupid" and "like an idiot" while encountering things in a situation that was new to me, but not new to many people. Being aware of my inexperience with this situation, even though I knew it was largely due to economic class issues beyond my control, only made me feel more embarrassed and inadequate. The therapist said to me, "There is a difference between ignorance and learning." Such wise advice! If we truly believe we are not being willfully ignorant, but are engaged in learning, even if it may be difficult terrain, then we are following a path of progress and love. The world is tough enough. Let's be kind to ourselves.

This is also a good time to mention the constraints and realities of economic class. In Peter Singer's book, *The Life You Can Save: How to Do Your Part to End World Poverty*,[5] he promotes the idea that people who live in wealthier countries have the ability to eradicate world poverty. This is based on most people giving five percent of their income to charity, although he believes people should actually donate a higher percentage. Within the book, he is very clear, however, that giving five percent is no hardship for someone earning $500,000, but may be tough for someone supporting a family in the United States on $50,000.[6] His focus is

---

5 Peter Singer, *The Life You Can Save: How to Do Your Part to End World Poverty* (New York, NY: Random House, 2010).

6 Singer, 162.

definitely on the "superrich." They obviously have the means to give more, which can eradicate more poverty at a quicker pace.

This same spirit of awareness of economic realities is part of Love Activism. All of us can be love activists and make profound positive changes, regardless of our level of income. For example, it takes courage, but no money, to join a protest march or intently listen to a suffering person's story. There are many practices mentioned in the book that require no money or very small amounts, but others may require funds that are not available if you are experiencing financial difficulties. This book is written for a wide audience, so simply focus on the activism you can perform within your means. There is absolutely never a reason to feel guilt or inadequacy.

Those reading this who are fortunate to have a good income, however, should ask themselves why they are not doing certain things. For example, let's say that recycled paper products cost more and you can afford them with little to no sacrifice, but you go for the less expensive ones. This would be something to examine. In Singer's book, he writes, "Do you have a bottle of water or a can of soda on the table beside you as you read this book? If you are paying for something to drink when safe drinking water comes out of the tap, you have money to spend on things you don't really need."[7] Although his statement may sound harsh, it really gave me pause when I read it. I found myself in his critique.

Who Are You!?

Before we begin to look deeper at defining love in the next chapter, I will tell you a little of my story that brought me to writing this book. If you are interested in this book, then you and I probably have a few things in common. I imagine we both wish to live our lives authentically. We want to work for a better world. We are horribly saddened by racism, sexism, homophobia, violence, and cruelty in our world. Still, you may be wondering, "Who is this person? How is she an expert on all of this?" These are perfectly reasonable questions!

From a young age, I was deeply concerned about injustice in the world and did not have much interest in materialism. At times this made me feel like an outsider. As a teenager in 1980s Southern California, I found a community of other outsiders who had beliefs similar to mine in

---

7 Singer, xi.

the punk rock scene. I became politicized through this. People involved with the punk rock scene had different experiences back then. For me, it felt like I was part of a vibrant protest movement. Through the lyrics of bands with a political message, such as the Dead Kennedys from San Francisco and Conflict from England, I developed my awareness of human and animal rights. I experienced a shift in consciousness that changed my life and continues to influence me. Ultimately, the possibility of living my life as a political statement was revealed.

Now, decades later and after a ton of hard work, endurance, and swimming through the debt of a bachelor's degree and two master's degrees, I find myself blessed to be a community college librarian and professor where I serve some of the most amazing students in the universe. A large part of me, however, is still the sixteen-year-old girl with a mohawk making anti-establishment art.

A few years ago, while in the middle of my life and feeling alienated and disillusioned by cruelty in the world, I thought a lot about activism. What did it mean to be an activist? If human history is full of injustices and people continue to find the need to get together in resistance, over and over again, how is progress ever truly made? It was out of this despair and thinking about love (which I'll elaborate on in the next chapter) that I created my version of activism called Love Activism. I made Love Activism cards with activism ideas that I gave out for a few years. Then I created hand-painted brochures and love activist art that I would sell at festivals. This led to more reflection on the depths of Love Activism, which ultimately resulted in what you are reading right now.

Although there is a need and a place for academic writing, I am also concerned about activist writing that is solely written for academics. I wish for my work to be approachable to as wide an audience as possible and more practical than theoretical. I hope I have succeeded and also hope you will find the book welcoming to you. *Love Activism* is part of my individual growth and understanding. You may not agree with all of my points. You may find flaws in my thinking that I may agree with if we were to have a discussion. It is true that what you are reading, although fixed for a moment at the time of publication, will always be a work-in-progress. Like all human creations, if I wait until everything is perfect, it will never be completed. At this time in my life, when I am approaching age fifty, this is my offering to you and my desire to put something positive out in the world. Thank you for your interest in exploring Love Activism.

Expanding Our Definition of Love

Before looking deeper at Love Activism's elements and practices, let's consider the importance of broadening our ideas of love. I recently attended a Day of Mindfulness at Deer Park Monastery, a Buddhist monastery in Escondido, California. The monk offering a talk spoke of the human difficulties of loneliness, anxiety, depression, and suffering. He mentioned how we often experience these emotions profoundly when dealing with romantic love. Our culture definitely has an obsession with romantic love and coupling. Sharon Salzberg, writing on "real love," affirms this: "Our minds are too often clouded by pop-culture images that equate love with sex and romance, delivered in thunderbolts and moonbeams....It makes us cling frantically to relationships that are bound to change, challenge us, or slip away."[1] Those living lives, even happy lives, without a traditional relationship or without being engaged in a panicked search for romantic love run the risk of being pitied or viewed as strange folk, which can cause self-doubt and anxiety. In her article, "Seeking the Comfort of an Old Flame: Solitude," Lisa Ko, though happy, displays this so well when she writes, "...I feared something was wrong with me for not wanting what everyone else did. It made me uncomfortable, like I became when people expressed concern that I was traveling alone."[2] We have become so accustomed to privileging one narrative.

---

1 Sharon Salzberg, "Real Love," *Tricycle*, Summer 2017, 26.

2 Lisa Ko, "Seeking the Comfort of an Old Flame: Solitude," *New York Times*, July 2, 2017, 5.

The artist Mary Stephenson had an experience at a wedding when she told another guest about how she has been a single woman for years. The stranger replied to her, "'What a waste.'"[3] We cannot tell the intent or exactly what the stranger's comment to Stephenson was supposed to convey, but describing her single status as "a waste" was clearly not a positive response. It suggested something was lacking and not being used to its fullest potential. It speaks to the obsession and value given to romantic love, which is most commonly presented as a man and a woman. Not only do we see it everywhere in movies, television shows, and advertisements, but people often want to know others' relationship statuses and will sometimes ask inappropriate, painful, or unwanted questions.

Once when I was close to thirty and working in an office with some women who married young and were in traditional marriages, two of the women came to my office one day to inquire on why I wasn't married yet and, "getting on with things." Even though I had a great job and was clearly happy and enjoying life, they thought something must be wrong with me. It hurt deeply to discover this after working with them for a few years.

Many years later, when I was married, I remember another instance where I attended a women's luncheon of mostly wealthy donors for my former dean. At the luncheon I discovered many of the women did not work and my career as a librarian was more of a curiosity. At one point, a woman at the table pointed to my wedding band and announced, "Oh, you're married! That's good!" It was as if that gave me credibility and the status to be there. I wasn't just the working woman. I was the *married* working woman, so I had instant value. It reminds me of a passage in Chimamanda Ngozi Adichie's *We Should All Be Feminists:* "I know an unmarried woman in Nigeria who, when she goes to conferences, wears a wedding ring because she wants her colleagues to – according to her – 'give her respect.'"[4] Adichie reflects on the sadness of the reality that a woman's worth may be diminished if she is not married.

These two examples above are just a sampling of the many times I've experienced something unpleasant or upsetting related to my relationship status or, more pointedly, my value depending on if I had or didn't have a man. It is important to acknowledge that these experiences are hurtful, but I'm still coming from a place of privilege as a heterosexual woman.

---

3 Aimee Farrell, "Art Matters: 'Boyfriends' as Lifelike Props, but Passive," *New York Times,* Feb. 19, 2017, 3.

4 Chimamanda Ngozi Adichie, *We Should All Be Feminists* (New York, NY: Anchor Books, 2015), 29.

I can only imagine the magnitude and painful navigation required for someone from the LGBTQ community who does not fit into the confines of heteronormativity.

Our preoccupation with romantic love and the elevation of it over other types of love appears in our everyday speech. This is highly evident in how the common phrase, "just friends" devalues friendship. Think of how many times, when asked if we are romantically involved with someone, that we respond, "No, we're just friends." Then consider how many times people described as "just friends" remain in our lives much longer than people we were involved with romantically. Indeed, a friendship can easily last a lifetime and outlive even several marriages.

It is important to make clear that I am not suggesting we should diminish romantic love or give up on it. The experience of romantic love can be a beautiful, uplifting, and mysterious thing. It contains a unique, seductive power. If we are fortunate, the experience of romantic love can be life-affirming. A strong romantic relationship can enrich our lives and be a supportive and nurturing space. What I am saying, however, is that by elevating this love or desperately chasing it, we can lose sight of all the other forms of love we have. Then, if we lose the romantic love, we may fall into such despair that we find ourselves inconsolable. Even if our despair is only temporary, it can be devastating and difficult to overcome. I have been there. For some, it can cause a closing of the heart, bitterness, and a longstanding loss of joy. We can protect ourselves from this by broadening our definition of love.

Let's Not Miss Out on All the Love

I first became interested in deeply contemplating the meaning of love beyond romantic love after being divorced for close to two years and having no interest in pursuing such a relationship. This was not out of bitterness or depression. The truth is that I found myself in the midst of an expansion of my creative life. Although I lived alone, I was not lonely. I was, as Lisa Ko experienced when writing about getting her own apartment, "…alone, so alone, and I had never been happier."[5] My life was peaceful and magical. I recall some of my students, when they found out I lived alone and did not have a partner or children, becoming very interested in my status. What did I do all the time? How could I be okay with my situation? How was I

---

5 Ko, "Seeking the Comfort of an Old Flame," 5.

fulfilled? But there I was in my beautiful one-bedroom apartment feeling like a millionaire. One of my former female students contacted me after graduating and told me that my happiness as a single woman gave her hope and possibilities she had not considered before.

Around this time, I started to think about all the different parts of my life that were connected to love. I read bell hooks' *All About Love*[6] and found that it captured so much of what I was feeling. I don't know anyone who writes so poignantly about love as hooks. In *All About Love*, she devotes one chapter to romantic love, but also writes of love in the context of spirituality, work, community, and more. I read this book alone and then with students and once again with a community reading group. It is interesting that I was thinking, reading, and writing about love so much at a time in my life when it may have appeared to others that I didn't have love. Yet, I felt no absence of love.

This progression in my thinking of love also occurred after reading several empowering memoirs by women who happened to live all or a major part of their lives outside of the conventional man-woman relationship paradigm. This included *Woodswoman* by Anne LaBastille,[7] Alice Koller's *An Unknown Woman: A Journey to Self-discovery*,[8] and an exquisite autobiography by Katharine Butler Hathaway titled, *The Little Locksmith*.[9] These women cultivated love and meaning in their lives through different avenues. I realized placing a hierarchy on types of love, and putting romantic love at the top of this hierarchy, is too limiting and has the potential to cause much suffering.

During this time I created a zine titled, *Love is the Greatest Search*. (Zines are self-published magazines, booklets, and pamphlets. See the Creativity chapter for more about zines). A few people seeing the title assumed it was about the search for romantic love. One man even told me he bought it to help him "figure out" what women want in a relationship, but, if he would have asked me, I would have explained it had nothing to do with that! The zine was about all the things I love in my life, such as traveling, books, music, and riding my bike. The idea behind it was to expand the awareness of how much love we have within various contexts and to help those who may feel love is absent from their life without a partner.

6 bell hooks, *All About Love: New Visions* (New York, NY: Perennial, 2001).

7 Anne LaBastille, *Woodswoman* (New York, NY: E. P. Dutton, 1976).

8 Alice Koller, *An Unknown Woman: A Journey to Self-discovery* (New York, NY: Holt, Rinehart and Winston, 1981).

9 Katharine Butler Hathaway, *The Little Locksmith* (New York, NY: Feminist Press, 2000).

Love in Action and Protest

It was within this way of thinking about love that I saw it as the main force behind what I began to think of as a living, daily activism. Once the concept of love was broadened, I saw how it applied to so many aspects of my life and how the simple questions of "Does this make me love more?" or "What does love want me to do?" could be perpetual points of departure for living a peaceful, kind life. Love may be hard to define, since it is something we think of more as an emotion or a feeling, but if we consider love in any context, it is when we wish for the person, group, community, or animal to prosper. When we love, we wish no harm for who we love. And, when we love and discover our actions or words are causing suffering we look for ways to change our behavior. Love exists in opposition to apathy. My commitment to political and social issues became part of this understanding of love. Ultimately, I determined that it was love that would save us. And, it had to be love in action. Love infused in our daily lives. Love as an act of protest. Radical love. Ultimately, what I came to call Love Activism. I believed, and continue to believe even more, that love as a direct action is what we need to overcome injustice. This means love starting with ourselves and stretching to encompass all living beings, our communities, and the natural world. It takes courage and commitment to live in this way, but the great thing about love is that each of us has infinite amounts of it inside of us. It is always there waiting for us. Let's get started on our journey.

The Eight Beautiful Elements of Love Activism

As my work and thinking with Love Activism grew, I came to realize that its strength is in its holistic nature. Over time and after meditating on the various pieces that construct this form of activism, I determined it has eight essential elements: service, hope, empathy, non-violence, self-care, creativity, feminism, and mindfulness. I made art pieces with corresponding circles of colors for the elements, which is why you will see colors listed at the beginnings of the chapters. Each element is unique, yet they overlap with each other and are part of the larger whole. For the most harmonious practice, all eight should be meditated on and become part of a thriving and joyful activist life. By embracing these elements, we make changes in our lives and move closer each day to a profound way of seeing others and our world with our hearts.

Service

Colors: yellow, orange, hint of gold

Service occurs when we perform acts of kindness for our loved ones, our communities, strangers, and the environment. Even what seems to be the simplest act of service can light someone's heart, which will also light our own. One way to think of the profound impact of service is to consider how you felt when someone did something for you without expecting anything in return.

I used to live in a large apartment complex where my good friend also lived. Once she knew I was very ill with a stomach ailment, so she went to the store and bought food and drink items she thought I may be able to have. Knowing I was in bad shape and likely sleeping, she sent me a text to let me know these things were at my door instead of calling or knocking. What she left me were not things I would normally buy, but she was right. Little by little, I ate what she brought and I felt better. These items would have been good medicine on their own, but the element of service that her gift was wrapped in, turned them into magical medicine. It's that warm feeling you get in your heart. I can remember other instances of something like this throughout my life when the food that was prepared for me or brought to me seemed like medicine. This experience is the miraculous nature of service as an act of love.

Work

When we think of our work, if we are self-employed or fortunate to be employed by individuals or an organization that respects us and isn't exploitative, we can imagine it as an opportunity to practice the element of service. Of course, when we consider service as a form of activism in the workplace, the ideas presented here cannot flourish in a workplace where people are subject to hostility and abuse. The practices discussed here are for healthy workplaces. Within a positive work setting, regardless of the exact position we hold, there are opportunities to serve others by being peaceful and reducing workplace drama; refraining from gossip; determining how we can help and support those we work with; and being kind and helpful to the public. If we do not interact directly with the public, but we produce tangible, practical objects or art as part of our work, this can also be viewed as a service offering. We can step away from routines and ask ourselves questions. How will what I am creating be used by others? How will what I am producing help the person who buys it? What will it mean for someone to have my art in their home?

We have all likely encountered someone who performs Love Activism through their work. This is the type of individual who is not just going through the motions, but one who understands the profound calling they have received to serve. One experience I will never forget involved a music therapist and my mom. It happened a few days before my mom passed away. She was in an intensive care unit after experiencing a massive stroke. This was after she had already suffered breast cancer and horrible complications from chemotherapy. In *How to Love,* Thich Nhat Hanh writes, "If we have happy parents, we have received the richest inheritance of all."[1] This really sums up my mom. Everyone who encountered her could see her bright light.

At the university where I used to work, we offered a degree in musical therapy, so I knew about the existence of this vocation, but I never encountered a music therapist until one day when I was sitting in the ICU next to my mom's bed. A music therapist came in the room with a harp and asked if she could play it for us. She had an amazing kindness and peaceful presence about her. My mom had been a singer her whole life and loved music. It is too painful to describe my mom's condition at the time, but something magical happened when she heard the harp. Her face looked ecstatic and glowing. Although it was impossible to understand my mom's speech those final days, when the therapist stopped playing the music, I asked my mom if she heard it. In a clear voice, she declared, "Oh, yes!" I started crying and the therapist came and put her arms around me. It was clear

---

1 Thich Nhat Hanh, *How to Love* (Berkeley, CA: Parallax Press, 2015), 106.

that her act of service was not just for the patients, but all who came in contact with her music.

As a love activist, a true blessing would be having a career in a service profession, such as the music therapist, that provides a strong, living wage. In *All About Love* bell hooks' writes, "Individuals who are able to be economically self-sufficient doing what they love are blessed. Their experience serves as a beacon to all of us, showing us the ways right livelihood can strengthen self-love, ensuring peace and contentment in the lives we lead beyond work."[2] This notion of "right livelihood" is an important one to consider.

During a visit to Deer Park Monastery, the Buddhist monastery I mentioned earlier, I was fortunate to participate in the Recitation of the Fourteen Mindfulness Trainings. I discovered the Eleventh Mindfulness Training is concerned with "Right Livelihood." It begins, "Aware that great violence and injustice have been done to our environment and society, we are committed not to live with a vocation that is harmful to humans or nature. We will do our best to select a livelihood that contributes to the wellbeing of all species on earth and helps realize our ideal of understanding and compassion."[3] This is one of the areas of Love Activism that may call on us to make a radical change. Consider your current work or desired work. Does the industry, company, corporation, or institution promote peace and justice? Is it harmful to humans, animals, and the earth or would you say it is neutral or helpful? If you believe it is mostly neutral, is this neutrality in accord with your activism? These are deep questions and ones we may be afraid to ask, but how we earn a living is definitely central to our lives as love activists. If we do not have a "right livelihood," but we are engaged in Love Activism, there is a disharmony and imbalance.

It is important to note that working in a profession as the music therapist or in other professional service careers, such as librarian, teacher, counselor/psychologist, and so on may not be accessible to everyone, due to various reasons. For example, years of education and professional credentials may require significant finances. To even embark on such a journey, one may need to come from an upper economic class or take out federal loans which could straddle an individual for decades or a lifetime. In the United States, undocumented individuals wanting to attend a university,

---

2 hooks, *All About Love*, 64.

3 Deer Park Monastery, *Mindfulness Trainings Recitation Booklet: The Two Promises, the Five and the Fourteen Mindfulness Trainings* (Escondido, CA, Deer Park Monastery, n.d.), 23.

even if they have been in the country from a very young age, may not have access to federal financial aid or other loans/grants. In addition, even securing such a job, once one has the credentials, may be incredibly difficult due to the competitive nature of the labor market. As mentioned at the beginning of this chapter, though, we must remember that we can practice service through all kinds of vocations and not just those that require specialized credentials.

Presence in Service

What do we mean by presence within the context of Love Activism? Consider how hurtful and frustrating it is when you believe you are having a conversation with someone and you realize the person is not paying attention. I have been an offender here. Once during a busy day, a student came to my office to have a discussion with me. She was talking for a few minutes when I realized my mind was preoccupied with the task I was trying to complete before she arrived. In fact, I recall my body was only half turned toward her. I made a gesture to interrupt her as politely as possible and apologized for my inattentiveness. I told her I had been distracted. I asked her if she would be willing to start over and I would give her my complete attention. Although I had been physically close to her and it may have seemed I was listening, I was not fully present at first.

There is a nun I used to visit for spiritual direction. When I would get to her office and sit down, she would always ask to take a few minutes to close our eyes and get grounded. I greatly appreciated this. Once we started talking, it always seemed that she was fully present with me. When we are serving others by visiting them or listening, we can practice techniques to increase our awareness and presence. This should be the case with strangers or close friends. We can turn off our phones or put them where we won't be tempted to look. If we are distracted at first, we can be honest about this and finish whatever it is we are doing before listening to the other person. We can take a deep breath before walking into a meeting to quiet our minds. Between clients or others in a service setting, if we are able to, we can close our eyes for a moment and then meet with the next person. Tchiki Davis suggests something like this called an "imagination break," where we sit for a moment and visualize our next encounter with a person as positive. She explains that the "brain has a difficult time differentiating between things that happen in your imagination and things that happen in real life."[4] This does not mean the interaction will go exactly as you intend, but you enter into a space feeling positive and present.

Many years ago I delivered books to homebound patrons through the local public library as a volunteer. I can't say I was always good at this, since I was often rushed, but it was obvious that some people looked forward to my visit as much as the books. This was not because of me. It was because they were lonely and wanted the company of another human being. There was one woman in particular who was direct in asking me to stay with her for awhile on several occasions. She was severely disabled and lived alone. One time I spent hours at her apartment helping her make a large collage of images she liked from old magazines. I wasn't my usual young and rushed self on that day, which is probably why I remember it so clearly. Because I slowed down and immersed myself in the project, being fully attentive, I had as much fun as her creating the collage.

With all of our various obligations, our time is so limited. When we give time to others by being fully present, we are giving one of the richest gifts we can offer. One of my least favorite expressions is "killing time." Life is too short to think of time in this way. There is always an opportunity to be fully present and realize the divine gift time is at any moment. Cultivating mindfulness, another of the eight beautiful elements of Love Activism we will look at later, can help us improve our ability to be present for others and ourselves. Then we will have no need for "killing time." We will only be spending our time well and becoming more present in our daily lives.

Vulnerability and Authenticity in Service

Authenticity and vulnerability could be commented on in other chapters, since they are so vital to Love Activism, but it seems that it is most fitting to reflect on these qualities here. This is because it is during practices of service that we may have personal contact with others that will be greatly enhanced if we are able to be not only present, but authentic and vulnerable.

Vulnerability can be understood in different ways and this depends on the context. One negative example is when an individual is put in a

---

4 Tchiki Davis, "How to Feel More Positive about Your Work," *Greater Good Magazine*, Nov. 30, 2017, http://greatergood.berkeley.edu/article/item/how_to_feel_more_positive_about_your_work

vulnerable position to be exploited and harmed. Another negative example is when someone is too vulnerable to be able to self-protect. These understandings of vulnerability are not to be embraced. The vulnerability I'm writing of here, which is a powerful and sometimes life-changing way to live, is a type of vulnerability that is cultivated and self-driven as a form of strength.

Many of us are afraid of being vulnerable. This is due to different reasons, such as our pride and the fact that we may have been hurt many times by people we trusted, so we build layers of protection over the years. In our culture, we often see vulnerability presented as something weak. We are supposed to be tough-as-nails and "not let anyone see us down." Competition is king and vulnerability rarely has a safe place when cutthroat competition is praised. There is also a fear that if others see our true selves, we will be rejected, so we put on different masks and act appropriately in our various roles. Maybe we have dark secrets that cause us pain, but we are unable to reveal ourselves and seek help. We may feel like divided selves acting in so many roles that our real selves are not seen by most people or possibly by no one. This is when authenticity comes into play. As we put on our masks to perform, what others see is inauthentic. I used to live this way. A day came in my life when I found myself completely exposed. It was terrifying, but opened me up to a new way of living that sees the strength in being both vulnerable and authentic. I will tell you a little of my story.

For several years, I appeared as someone with a successful marriage and career. I was involved locally and nationally in my profession, especially in feminism and women's studies. I was the chair of the largest division at my library. I taught classes, traveled to conferences to give presentations, and was successfully building my publishing record. I spoke well of my husband to everyone. The truth was that I was living a double life. My life at home was unpredictable, abusive, and often terrifying. It wasn't like that at first, of course; it was a gradual thing that developed over several years until I realized I was trapped and in danger. Due to threats, I truly believed I would be physically harmed if I left.

During this time in my life, it always felt like there were different pots cooking on the stove. Most were happily simmering along, but there was one big pot that was almost boiling over. That was my abusive marriage. My hand was on that lid, trying to keep the contents from pouring out and ruining everything I worked so hard for. When I recall what I endured at times while at home, even all these years later, I can still feel sick and traces of shame and embarrassment creep in. On many occasions,

I would experience threats and horrific verbal abuse over the phone while away from home, only to walk into a work meeting or classroom or gathering of friends a few minutes later with a smile on my face, but with my stomach churning and my heart rapidly beating. On the surface, no one could tell anything was wrong. One time I came very close to confiding in a colleague. At the last minute, I pulled back out of fear for my reputation. What would she think of me, the supposed grand feminist who was secretly being abused by her husband? I felt like a fraud. My situation was a painful and shameful secret. I spent so much time and mental energy trying to figure out how I could escape without being killed or anyone finding out. Then a weekend of terror occurred, a moment I feared may happen, and I was able to trick my husband and escape in my car. I knew the end had arrived and I would not return. I knew the police and courts would be involved. And I knew everyone was going to find out the truth about me.

When this all occurred, I imagined people would judge me and find me weak. I believed no one would want to associate with me. There are myths that this type of abuse does not happen to "strong" people. I'm sure that some people may have thought things about me, due to a lack of understanding about the complexities of domestic violence and the cycle of abuse, but what I discovered overwhelmed me. My friends and colleagues, though initially shocked, understood and offered incredible support. They even thought I was strong for leaving. They only wanted to help me. In becoming absolutely vulnerable, I was free of my painful secret. A difficult and courageous path was still ahead for me and I continue to struggle at times with memories of what I experienced, but I no longer live a divided life. Maybe you have experienced a transformation like me and you know the intense healing that comes when you stand exposed, all of your masks gone, and you receive love and support.

This experience of vulnerability profoundly changed how I interact with students, friends, and strangers. It has allowed me to offer a practice of service I was not able to before. For example, in the past, if someone spoke to me about abuse they experienced or if domestic violence came up as a topic in a classroom discussion, I was deeply empathetic, but I would never reveal my story. I'm not suggesting that we should always reveal private and difficult things. We need to take care of ourselves and be mindful enough to know our own balance between public and private life and what we are comfortable with sharing in different circumstances. It just happened in my life that in most situations admitting to others that I have been abused has allowed me to help others more. This level of vulnerability and authenticity has expanded well beyond that painful story into other opportunities, especially in my work with students.

One evening a student called me late from her dorm room. She had transferred from the community college where I work to a large, prestigious university. She would soon be the first person in her family to graduate from college, which is a background I share with her and many of my students. When she called me, she wanted to know if I ever felt like her. One question she asked was, "Have you ever felt lonely?" Not only did I respond, "God, yes!," but I gave examples and even revealed that I can still experience loneliness. During this call, I also spoke honestly about having felt other emotions she was struggling with. I believe taking her call was a practice of service, but being vulnerable and authentic made it more meaningful for both of us. I have received so much positive feedback from students that I believe embracing authenticity and vulnerability is a movement toward radical love. When we are serving others, how beautiful it is if we are our true selves, allowing others to see we have scars and complex, difficult lives, too. It gives others a safe resting space and permission to be their true selves. I am also hopeful that by living authentically and vulnerably we will allow other people to break free from silence and shame.

Serving Animals and the Earth

If we agree that all things are connected, our understanding of service will broaden beyond human beings to include non-human animals and the earth. Sometimes I have heard people get angry when others want to help non-human animals. This comes from a belief that this will take away from human rights work. In my experience, many people who are animal and environmental rights activists are also very engaged in human rights work. We do not need to narrow our understanding of service, but broaden it, keeping in mind the interconnectedness and lack of hierarchies in Love Activism. Besides, helping the natural world ultimately helps human beings. There is no separation, but a direct correlation.

In *The Earth Path: Grounding Your Spirit in the Rhythms of Nature*, Starhawk writes, "We can make personal choices that reduce the greenhouse gases we each produce. It's important that we do this not out of a sense of guilt or resentful obligation, but as an affirmative choice to more deeply integrate our values and our everyday actions."[5] When we think of service in this capacity, how rich our practices can be. Some questions we may ask ourselves as a starting point are: How much in harmony is my life with the natural world? What acts of service could I perform that help the environment? Are there things I have knowledge of that I could do on a larger-scale or community level to bring this type of service to others, such as teaching people how to grow their own food or teaching others about the best plants to grow to help the natural world thrive?

Starhawk also provides the following wise advise: "The rising of the ocean from global warming is ultimately more real, and more important to the web of life on the planet, than the rising of stock prices or profit margins. The complex exchange of nutrients in the soil is more vital to life on earth than any negotiated trade agreement."[6] If her statement resonates with you, it is easy to see why our activism must be an interconnected practice.

While discussing service within the context of animals and the environment, there is also much evidence of the healing nature of animal companions. The relationship is mutually therapeutic. In *Paws & Effect: The Healing Power of Dogs*, Sharon Sakson reports on how the "steady presence" of dogs has been shown to reduce blood pressure. She also writes on the strong bond between animals and children with mental or physical disabilities, as well as the life-changing impact that caring for a dog can have on prisoners.[7] Service as an act of love could involve contributing to food drives that include food for poor people's cats and dogs. We could walk dogs for elderly people in our community. We could provide foster homes for abused or neglected animals, especially those who are older and have less of a chance of being adopted. All of these acts of service only broaden our circle of compassion. I have experienced this.

If you have adopted and cared for an older animal, you will surely relate to my story of Joni. From the beginning, the adoption of Joni taught me lessons. After living in apartments for all of my adult life, which made having a dog difficult, one of my dreams, if I was fortunate to live in a house, was to adopt a German Shepherd. In my mind, for many years, I saw the tan and black German Shepherd I would adopt and I already had the name picked out: Hannah. When the time came, I fell in love

---

5 Starhawk, *The Earth Path: Grounding Your Spirit in the Rhythms of Nature* (New York, NY: Harper Collins, 2005), 94.

6 Starhawk, 14.

7 Sharon Sakson, *Paws & Effect: The Healing Power of Dogs* (New York, NY: Alyson Books, 2007), 8.

with a seven-year-old white German Shepherd, nothing like the imagined Hannah. The shelter thought she would never find a home. This was because of her tendency to back up and be afraid of human beings. I was told she was a "loner" and would probably not be a good companion. She was at the rescue's shelter for eight months. They offered to show me other dogs, but my heart was already pinned to her.

Once we were home, the name I had ready for years didn't work. Instead, I named her Joni. I quickly realized that much of what I thought would happen, my various expectations for how my life with a dog would be, needed to be adjusted. Although Joni is sweet and has never demonstrated aggressiveness, she remains cautious of everyone, except for me, so she is not really able to socialize with others. She likes to be around my friends – just at a distance. She has a tremendous fear of fireworks and thunderstorms and cannot be left alone with these loud sounds. She will also sometimes be in what I call "one of her moods" and act anxious for reasons I cannot determine. Still, she has definitely come a long way from how she was when I first brought her home, but I understand that things that happened to her earlier in life cannot be entirely erased from her memory. Instead of remaining rigid in my expectations of how I want her to be, I accept and love her for who she is. In a strange way, because I experienced abuse, I can relate to her. What others may consider her shortcomings are reasons I love her more.

Fig 1

This relationship is one of the most profound of my life. (Fig. 1 shows me with Joni on the second anniversary of her adoption.) Ultimately, they were wrong at the shelter. She is a great companion, following me around in the garden, howling her beautiful greeting when I come home, and sleeping in my bedroom each night. Caring for her, which could be viewed as a form of service, brings me great joy. It is true that Joni teaches me about love every day. She has even enriched my life as an activist by expanding my ability to forgive and accept.

Practices of Service: cook a meal for your friend or partner; visit the ill; take someone to a medical appointment; clean or make repairs for someone; provide literacy tutoring; bring food to the poor and their companion animals; mail books to prisoners; volunteer to clean litter at the ocean or other natural area; mail someone a surprise postcard; walk dogs at a shelter or for elderly or disabled neighbors with limited mobility; start a community reading group; be an advocate for foster youth; call or visit someone who may be lonely; adopt an old animal; grow plants that help the environment thrive; visit cats at a shelter…

Empathy

Colors: light blue, sky blue, white

Empathy is a deep form of compassion. When we are empathetic, we do not just know about or relate to another's pain or suffering, but we feel the pain and suffering deeply as if it were our own. There are actions we can practice that allow us to cultivate and expand this beautiful element.

Presence in Empathy

In the previous chapter on service, we looked at the importance of presence. Presence is also a key aspect of empathy. I became deeply aware of this when I was working on an oral history project that involved meeting with women, often in their homes, to listen to their stories. I realized from these interactions that not just the telling of a personal story was an act of social justice, but so was the listening. If no one listens, this is an act of silencing another's voice. I also became aware of the ethical issues involved in listening. We need to take care of the stories we receive and accept them with gratitude, realizing they are gifts.

We can think of being fully present while listening to someone's story as a form of witnessing. This act of witnessing, of not turning away or tuning out, but being fully present, is Love Activism. This deep listening also allows us to be more compassionate and understanding (see the Mindfulness chapter for more about deep listening). For example, listening to a story from someone with a background or experiences unlike your own can profoundly change how you may feel about entire groups of people. It awakens our empathy. Some people, such as celebrities and those with power, especially historically, have large audiences for their stories. Also, they do not get to tell their stories just one time, but many times and may even be paid or receive more fame from their personal stories. If you are the listener of a story from someone who will likely never have their story heard by others, imagine how important your presence is. You are truly blessed by this unique gift.

One of the most amazing depictions of empathy and the importance of presence occurs in the documentary, *The Artist is Present*.[1] The film captures the performance art of Marina Abramovic during an installation at the Museum of Modern Art in New York City in 2010. As Abramovic sat in a chair in the gallery, people waited in line to sit in front of her. It was a one-on-one interaction in silence. People could sit for as long as they like. It was very successful in terms of people wanting to participate. People of all ages and backgrounds waited in long lines for the opportunity to sit in a chair across from her. Abramovic explains, "I was there, one hundred per-cent – three hundred percent – for each person. I became extremely recep-tive."[2] In the film many people are shown crying as they sit in silence with her. Abramovic continues, "What I found, immediately, was that the people sitting across from me became very moved. From the beginning, people were in tears – and so was I. Was I a mirror? It felt more than that. I could see and feel people's pain."[3] How often do we truly sit, without internal and external distractions, and really look at each other?

Even if we are not physically present, as in the examples of my oral history project or *The Artist is Present* performance piece, there are ways we can perform deep listening. This could be through reading interviews or memoirs or listening to oral histories through online collections such as *StoryCorps* or *The Moth Radio Hour*. Studs Terkel's classic book, *Working*,[4] provides insights into the lives of individuals in various jobs in the United States. Other examples are the first-person stories found in the social jus-tice books published by the Voice of Witness organization.[5] The narratives

---

1 *The Artist is Present*, directed by Matthew Akers (2012; USA: HBO Documentary Films, 2012), DVD.

2 Marina Abramovic, *Walk through Walls: A Memoir* (New York, NY: Crown Archetype, 2016), 309.

3 Abramovic, 309.

4 Studs Terkel, *Working: People Talk about What They Do All Day and How They Feel about What They Do* (New York, NY: The New Press, 2014).

5 Visit the Voice of Witness organization website at http://voiceofwitness.org/ to discover the se-ries of books they publish and the work they do that intersects personal narratives and social justice activism.

captured in these books cover the lives of undocumented individuals in the United States; the falsely imprisoned; and those suffering from war, economic struggles, and other injustices. (For more about the work of Voice of Witness, see my interview with Cliff Mayotte in the "Living Portraits: Interviews with Activists" section.) By spending focused time with reading or listening, we can expand our circle of compassion and empathy.

Empathy as Inclusive

When you are a member of an oppressed group, much strength, progress, and healing can arise out of identity politics. Through this practice, at its most intense level, people's political practice is solely based on a group they identify with. It is important to note that there are also some limitations here. Writing on identity politics, the late poet, teacher, and activist June Jordan stated, "Traditional calls to 'unity' on the basis of only one of these factors – race or class or gender – will fail, finally, and again and again, I believe, because no simple one of these components provides for a valid fathoming of the complex individual."[6] Jordan's thinking was too compassionate and too large for borders. In one of her most powerful essays, "The Hunters and the Hunted," Jordan, who was a bisexual woman of color, writes of going to a synagogue in an act of solidarity after a horrific shooting at a Jewish community center in Los Angeles by a white supremacist. Although she was not Jewish, in the final line of the essay, she calls out to the killer, "'Are you hunting for Jews? You're looking for me!'"[7] Through her inclusive activism, she identified with all of the oppressed.

Empathy as Love Activism is an inclusive practice. Being inclusive also allows us to be aware of intersecting identities, as Jordan mentioned above in her example of race, class, and gender. Once at a conference I saw a woman speak on how hard it was for her to find community. She was lesbian, so she did not feel fully accepted by heterosexual individuals. She was a larger size than the strict and cruel rules that govern weight and "beauty" in many Western cultures, which led to other issues of acceptance. She was vegan, so she was often ridiculed for this and felt out of place at gatherings, such as lesbian and gay gatherings where she expected to find support.

6 June Jordan, *Life as Activism: June Jordan's Writings from The Progressive*, ed. Stacy Russo (Sacramento, CA: Litwin Books, 2014), 8.

7 Jordan, 220.

When she went to vegan gatherings, some insensitive people offered her unsolicited weight loss advice. The list goes on and on. No matter where she turned, something was "wrong" and clashed with the different groups' identities. All of this suffering led her to thinking about the importance and compassion of inclusivity. This is what Jordan wrote about when she stated, "There is another realm of possibility: political unity and human community based upon concepts that underlie or supersede relatively immutable factors of race, class, and gender: the concept of justice, the concept of equality, the concept of tenderness."[8] May we be as brave as Jordan. May we be so courageous to embrace an inclusive empathy in our lives as activists.

Empathy for Animals

In the film, *The Wild Parrots of Telegraph Hill*,[9] we see the transformation of a man, Mark Bittner, through his love and care for a wild flock of parrots in San Francisco. At one moment in the film, he tells the story of Tupelo, an ill bird who came to him for comfort the night before the bird died. From this experience with Tupelo, Bittner determines he will no longer deny his love of the birds to others. One could argue it also represents a breakthrough in his understanding of his masculinity. He is no longer concerned about false notions of how he must appear as a man. I believe his transformation is a beautiful example of empathy between different species. As with the element of service, we do not need to feel limited. If an animal is suffering and in need of care, the empathy we feel is authentic and what we do in the situation can be a representation of our activism.

A personal story that illustrates empathy occurred when I visited a wildlife park in Central Florida many years ago with my mom. We went there assuming it was a wildlife refuge that cared for animals native to the area. I do recall seeing some injured animals that were cared for, but then I discovered other things. While walking around, we came across an African hippopotamus named Lu. A hippo in Central Florida? Yes, there he was, the only one of his kind, moving around in the water area of his enclosure, which was far from his real home. Much later I discovered he had been

---

8 Jordan, 9.

9 *The Wild Parrots of Telegraph Hill*, directed by Judy Irving (2005; New York, NY: Docurama), DVD.

used in entertainment early in his life, including in a Union Carbide commercial, but was now retired at the park. At one point while standing there with a group of people who were also watching Lu, he came out of the water. When he did, a horrible smell came with him. All of a sudden many of the people started laughing. I looked at the crowd laughing and then I saw my mom next to me. We were both silent. Later I asked her why she didn't laugh. "Because there was nothing funny about it," she said, "It was sad." I have reflected on this experience over the years. Once I told a friend about it. I asked him if he understood why it was so sad to see Lu alone and he responded, "Yes. That is what a heart is for."

Of course, we have no way of knowing if Lu is aware of his situation. I have heard that he is well-loved and cared for, which is much to be thankful for. Obviously, once he was done being used for entertainment purposes, the outcome could have been considerably worse. I also imagine there was never a possibility of him returning to his home in Africa, because of the way he was removed from his natural world. He would not survive there. People travel to see him and he is celebrated. He has lived a long life. Maybe he is happy, but we can't really know. We can allow ourselves to visualize other ways to treat animals, so that these outcomes are no longer a part of our reality. If this story of Lu, imagining him alone at the park, speaks to you, you may consider how empathy for animals can play a role in your activism. You may also reflect on the need to support sanctuaries for animals while boycotting zoos or wildlife parks that primarily function as venues for entertainment and viewing at the expense of peace and respect for all life. That is what a heart is for.

Caring For Yourself While Practicing Empathy

If you believe you are already an empathetic person, then you may be aware that it is important to draw boundaries and make sure you care for yourself as much as you care for others. Once when discussing this need for self-care with a friend, she gave the example of how you are instructed to put on your own oxygen mask during an airplane incident before assisting others. It is imperative to understand what empathy is not. It should not be self-destructive and it should not turn into co-dependence. Once this occurs, the element of self-care that is so important to Love Activism is being denied.

I recently read an article in the *New York Times Magazine* about a department at the White House that receives letters addressed to the president.[10] This article focused on letters sent to former president Barack Obama. An astonishing 10,000 letters and messages arrived daily. Many of these letters told tragic personal stories that emotionally impacted the readers. The author writes, "The letters could take a toll." In fact, monthly counseling sessions were offered "to anyone who felt the need."[11] One individual who was tasked with handling some of the difficult letters, "often needed a break from the unbearable sadness,"[12] so he would take care of himself by leaving his solitary work and instead hang out in the room where a group read together. This need for relief from sadness reminded me of my former work as a vocational rehabilitation counselor.

At my old job, almost daily, I read of someone's suffering through stacks of medical reports, surgical records, and psychological evaluations. I also had long in-person sessions with my clients, lasting from three to seven hours, where I talked with them and administered a series of tests. Many of my clients were men who suffered catastrophic injuries from various types of accidents. Some had missing limbs and many suffered from traumatic brain injuries that required extensive cognitive retraining. They were often depressed and almost always in pain. Their lives had changed significantly. I did this job for about six years. It was a highly rewarding experience, because I was provided an opportunity to help people, if only for a brief moment in time, with their suffering. During these years, I made sure to take good care of myself. I never missed a lunch break. I went to a café and bookstore for lunch every day where I relaxed and read before going back to the office. My bosses were also incredibly compassionate people toward the clients and the employees. They brought a yoga instructor to the office for us twice a month and my boss found out what magazine I liked and paid for a personal subscription to come to my home. There were many Fridays where we were told to close up early and get on with enjoying our weekend. All of these actions spoke to the need for caring for ourselves so that we could take care of others better.

Of course, there are times where we may find ourselves needing to sacrifice to help another, but it is important to check in with ourselves and not disregard our own health. In Robin Stern and Diana Divecha's article, "How to Avoid the Empathy Trap," they write, "The art of empathy

---

10 Jeanne Marie Laskas. "The Mailroom," (January 22, 2017). *The New York Times Magazine*, Jan. 22, 2017.

11 Laskas, 32.

12 Laskas, 33.

requires paying attention to another's needs without sacrificing one's own."[13] Handing over your life and wellbeing are not examples of empathy. When I was experiencing guilt over the aftermath of my abusive marriage, specifically my decision to leave someone who I believed had a mental illness, a wise person gave me Mary Oliver's poem, "The Journey." In this poem, we see someone being asked to mend things in a chaotic house that is "terrible" and trembling. Ultimately, the person leaves being "determined to save / the only life you could save."[14] After reading this poem, the wise person said to me, "You saved the only life you could save. It just happened that the life was your own." In the poem, the individual setting out on the journey recognizes her own voice and this voice becomes a companion. It speaks to the importance of not losing your powerful voice and intuition. Stern and Divecha's discussion of the "empathy trap" mentioned above reminds us that "emotional intelligence always requires being empathic with yourself. And that paradoxically allows you to be even more present for those you love."[15] A balance is necessary. As activists wanting to practice radical compassion, we need to include ourselves in this vision. (Please see the chapter on self-care for more reflections on caring for ourselves.)

Practices of Empathy: listen deeply to someone's story; read memoirs and oral histories of individuals with experiences both similar and different from you; do not judge another's suffering; think kind thoughts or pray for those in need; boycott circuses or places that use animals for entertainment; volunteer to answer calls on a suicide hotline; study and read about racism and other forms of injustice; meditate on how you would feel in another's difficult situation; look into self-help practices to maintain your balance and wellbeing...

---

13 Robin Stern and Diana Divecha. "How to Avoid the Empathy Trap," *University of California, Berkeley Greater Good Science Center.* July 7, 2015, http://greatergood.berkeley.edu/article/item/how_to_avoid_the_empathy_trap

14 Mary Oliver, "The Journey," in *Devotions: The Selected Poems of Mary Oliver* (New York, NY: Penguin Press, 2017), 350.

15 Stern and Divecha, "How to Avoid the Empathy Trap."

Hope

Colors: turquoise, deep blue, hint of gold

Hope brings us out of despair, even when we may see so much around us that suggests our activism makes no difference. Rebecca Solnit writes books on beautiful, wonderful topics, including walking, getting lost, feminism, and, yes, hope. In *Hope in the Dark: Untold Histories, Wild Possibilities*, she writes, "Your opponents would love you to believe that it's hopeless, that you have no power, that there's no reason to act, that you can't win. Hope is a gift you don't have to surrender, a power you don't have to throw away" (xi).[1] Hope is essential for an activist life.

Several studies speak to the importance of hope in overall well-being. In regards to education Vicki Zakrzewski states, "having hope may actually predict a student's future academic achievement *more* than having feelings of self-worth or a positive attitude towards life actually do."[2] Hope, along with gratitude, are described as significant concepts within happiness studies, according to Andrew Howell, Thomas Bailie, and Karen Buro, since "both are associated with well-being."[3] Another study by Simon Bury, Michael Wenzel, and Lydia Woodyatt[4] focused on sports, but reminds

1 Rebecca Solnit, *Hope in the Dark: Untold Histories, Wild Possibilities* (Chicago, IL: Haymarket Books, 2016), xi.

2 Vicki Zakrzewski, "How to Help Students Develop Hope," *Greater Good Magazine*, Nov. 6, 2012, https://greatergood.berkeley.edu/article/item/how_to_help_students_develop_hope

3 Andrew J. Howell, Thomas Bailie, and Karen Buro, "Evidence for Vicarious Hope and Vicarious Gratitude," *Journal of Happiness Studies* 16, (2015):688.

4 Simon Bury, Michael Wenzel, and Lydia Woodyatt. "Giving Hope a Sporting Chance: Hope as Distinct from Optimism When Events are Possible but Not Probable," *Motivation and Emotion* 40, (2016): 588.

me of activism, particularly activist efforts to confront issues that may feel insurmountable, such as systemic racism or rape culture. The study revealed that when a situation is most dire people will particularly invoke hope when they strongly believe in the outcome they desire. Hope, then, lives in the present, but is focused on changing those present circumstances into something better. Considering all of this, how do we create a feeling of hopefulness when faced with despair? One of the best ways to generate hope is to perform acts that propel us toward possibilities and a better future.

Cultivating Hope

In mindfulness practices, as we will discuss later in the book, we bring our focus to the present moment instead of living in fear of the future or out of regret and fear generated from the past. Still, I believe we can be actively aware and peaceful in the present moment while also creating a hopeful future. To do this, we can create things of hope to place around us. So, essentially, these creations live with us in the present day and generate hope.

One example of this practice is the creation of a vision board. A vision board can be created in a similar way as a collage, by pasting images and words from old books and magazines onto cardboard or another surface. A collage, however, can be created with or without a theme; a vision board is created with a clear intention. The intention could be to heal from a traumatic incident or manifest something such as peace or happiness in our lives. The intention could also be beyond us. As a love activist, you may feel passionate about creating a vision board that imagines a world free of racism or another dream that you deeply desire. An additional idea is to create a vision board tied to a personal goal that may be attainable in the near future. After I was blessed with my current position that provides me with a good salary, a dream of having a house materialized for me. I created a vision board while living in my former apartment that contained images and words I identified with this future home I wanted to have (fig. 2). The important thing to keep in mind is that the vision board should not represent something we must attain or we will be angry or depressed. It should represent possibilities without having a negative attachment. In this way, the vision board is not only a practice of hope, but a practice of self-care. It should make you feel good in your life today.

In addition or instead of a vision board, you may consider the simple act of making lists of hope. I have found this practice incredibly helpful.

Fig 2

When I was in a difficult place and I was not sure about my future, I made a list titled, "Places to Visit and Other Possibilities." I put this list in a place where I could see it all the time. Anyone visiting me at my old apartment also saw it. It was almost like a private, yet public, demonstration of hope and my desire to carry on and make it through. I no longer have this list and I know there are several places on it that I may not make it to, but the point is that it provided a message of hope.

I believe hope is tied to resilience. Other people can demonstrate this for us. Another thing I did around the time I had the list of places to visit was making something I called "The Inspiring Women Panels." I found photos online of various women who inspire me through their activism and art. I glued the photos on small individual pieces of wood that I painted different colors and then placed them on a string. Essentially, what I created was a garland of hope and resiliency through the images of these women. I hung it above my kitchen sink.

Home altars are another manifestation of hope. You do not need to follow a traditional religion to create your altar or even think of it as a spiritual exercise, unless you desire to. Similar to a vision board, but with tangible objects gathered together in a display, your altar can cultivate hope when you sit in front of it or even walk by as you go about your day. Focused on your life as an activist, you may assemble pieces and images that symbolize the peaceful and just world you are working toward.

If these ideas of vision boards, lists, women's panels, and altars do not speak to you, they may still inspire you to think of what you can place around your home or work area to signify hope. It is no small thing to create positive, daily reminders.

Gardening

Recently I was at a nursery to investigate purchasing some plants. I knew that rain and cooler weather was coming up, so I wasn't sure about the right ones to plant. I asked a man about some flowering plants and he responded, "They will be fine! They have had thousands of years to adapt. We think we are so tough!" Of course there are many parts of our natural world that have not been able to adapt to climate change, but when this man said this I looked at the small, dainty flowers with admiration. What a message of hope they were! Shortly after planting them, major winds came. I was not anticipating this and worried they would not make it, but they pulled through and are thriving. How resilient they are! I keep remembering what that man said.

I have noticed so many things since I have started to grow a garden of my own. I see patterns in nature I didn't notice before. Some plants have not made it and others that appeared to be doing poorly all of a sudden turned around and are vibrant and healthy. I'm thankful that I was patient and waited. I now understand that they were possibly going through a cycle or maybe they were not well, but rain, attention, or something more mysterious that I don't understand healed them.

Planting a garden is an amazingly hopeful thing we can do. We do not need a large plot of land to try this. Even in a small apartment there may be patio or window space to begin a garden using containers. My dad, a former farm boy who found himself living in an urban apartment, would grow vibrant tomato plants with only a tiny plot of dirt. If you would like more space to experiment than you have, look into getting a plot at a community garden. This will also give you the chance to work alongside people who are creating hope. You can plant things for beauty and aroma that will attract bees and butterflies. You may try to grow your own herbs and food as an act of hope, sustainability, and resistance. If something does not work out, simply try again. Always remember that there is a difference between learning and ignorance. Learning is tied to a forward momentum and hope; ignorance is stagnant and fearful.

All of these thoughts on gardening point to its amazing nature and far-reaching impact. Not only does it cultivate hope, but gardens also provide ways for us to practice several of the other beautiful elements of Love Activism, including self-care, creativity, and mindfulness. Service may also be a significant result of gardening, since we may bring beauty and food to our homes and communities.

The Importance of Anchors

Another way to cultivate hope is to have anchors in our life. When we think of anchors for a boat, we imagine something that helps to keep the boat from drifting. If we are feeling unsettled and disillusioned in our activism, it is important to not drift into depression, burn out, or resignation. We can metaphorically throw anchors out toward the future to chart a path. As our boat moves along, we can pick up each anchor and continue on to the next one. I believe it is important to always look ahead and make plans for positive things, even if we do not feel like it at the moment. Examples of this include writing possibilities in our calendars for future events. These may be events directly related to activism in the community, such as a protest march or gathering, or they could be things of a more personal nature. Examples of the latter are registering for a class or one-day workshop, making a note in our calendar of an art event at a museum, or getting advance tickets for a concert. Being a major book lover, when I hear of a book coming out, I write it on my calendar and look forward to the book's release. Some of these things may seem small, but they are not. They propel us toward a future where we can always see something on the horizon.

Practices of Hope: smile at strangers; plant a tree; join a community garden or start gardening at home; start reading a great, big book; enroll in a class you always wanted to take; reflect on the positive outcome of a loving act you performed; make a gratitude or future possibilities list you can refer to daily; create an altar or peaceful place; list future inspiring events on a calendar; create a vision board…

Non-Violence

Colors: deep violet, magenta, hint of gold

Non-violence is an essential practice for a compassionate life. Verbal assaults, not just physical acts, are forms of violence. We must consider all acts of violence in our lives that we are complicit in supporting and move toward eradicating them. This includes purchases we make, our speech, eating food that comes from violence, or performing customs and rituals that our culture may celebrate, such as hunting, that result in killing a living being.

Forms of Violence

A definition of violence is often limited to physical assault, but the insidious nature of violence comes in many forms. The Violence Prevention Alliance provides one definition: "the intentional use of physical force or power, threatened or actual, against oneself, another person, or against a group or community, that either results in or has a high likelihood of resulting in injury, death, psychological harm, maldevelopment, or deprivation."[1] Some key terms in this definition are "power" and "psychological harm," since they point to violence coming from a person in a position of authority, which could also be understood as a place of privilege, as well as the fact that violence may be something that does not cause a visible

---

1 Violence Prevention Alliance, "Definition and Typology of Violence," *World Health Organization*, 2018, http://www.who.int/violenceprevention/approach/definition/en/

physical injury or require physical contact. Obviously, if we simply consider the common knowledge that stress has been tied to health issues, it is easy to see how threats, verbal assaults, and hateful speech, including racist and sexist jokes, may not only hurt someone emotionally, but cause great physical harm over time. Love activists work to eradicate all such forms of violence from their lives, including condoning such "jokes," which may be portrayed as innocent humor, but only perpetuate stereotypes, contribute to the normalization of racism, dehumanize the "other," and objectify women, which can lead to misogyny and attitudes of acceptance towards physically harming women.

Lisa Feldman Barrett, a professor of psychology at Northeastern University has written on the impact of certain types of speech. Her research demonstrates that "words can have a powerful effect on your nervous system. Certain types of adversity, even those involving no physical contact, can make you feel sick, alter your brain – even kill neurons – and shorten your life."[2] It is something many of us know intuitively. If you have been the victim of verbal abuse or been forced to hear "jokes" in a setting where you did not have the opportunity to leave or you did not feel safe enough to object, you may have experienced strong bodily reactions, such as shakiness, upset stomach and nausea, or even something worse. This demonstrates that you do not need to be physically attacked to actually experience physical harm. Unfortunately, with social media and the current political climate, cruel and hateful speech has become a part of our daily lives, even if we are not a victim of it by someone in our workplace or home.

To advocate against this, be strong and do not participate in speech and jokes that promote outright cruelty, bigotry, and hate. When safe, leave such conversations. Self-reflect and consider if there are any forms of speech you have considered "innocent fun" and even promote yourself, that could be harmful. All of us can be victims of violence, but we are also well aware of individuals in our culture, such as members of the LGBTQ community, who suffer greatly from violence. Jokes that dehumanize these communities only add to a culture of hate. A saying that may help in our self-reflection is the following: "If you propose to speak, always ask yourself: Is it true? Is it necessary? Is it kind?" We can always look for where love is present in our speech and actions.

---

2 Lisa Feldman Barrett, "When Is Speech Violence?," *New York Times*, July 16, 2017, 9.

Veganism

I recently saw a pamphlet advocating veganism that said something to the effect of the following on the cover: "If you love animals and believe they should live peaceful lives, you are already a vegan at heart." This is simple, yet very true. As human beings though, we may have generations of cultural norms, peer pressure, and today's fast-paced society that unfortunately puts convenience at the center of many decisions, including food, over ethics, healthiness, and compassion. While working on this book, someone familiar with it, a feminist who works in an activist setting, asked me, "Don't you think your idea that eating animals is a form of violence will alienate some readers?" When I heard this, I considered that many ideas in this book, not just veganism, may alienate some readers, but my intent is not to alienate, it is to present my beliefs and invite others into a discussion and self-reflection of how to live a life as a peaceful activist. This may mean that some practices I advocate may not receive a warm response from all readers. I am very much aware, since I am vegan, that veganism is something that causes people discomfort, even though they may be awesome activists in other ways. If you feel yourself beginning to feel defensive or angry, I only ask that you reflect deeply and honestly on why that is and hang in there with me for the next several paragraphs.

Being vegan is an amazing form of activism that allows you to take a stand against violence on a daily basis and at every meal. Thich Nhat Hanh writes about the violence that can be intertwined with what we eat. The good news is that we can make choices. "With each meal," he states, "we make choices that help or harm the planet. 'What shall I eat today' is a very deep question."[3] Choosing veganism serves as a frequent and beautiful reminder of your commitment to peace for yourself and all living beings. I once overheard an animal rights activist say something to the effect of "what is at the end of your fork is a political statement." This is true in many ways, as we will see now concerning nonhuman animals and later in this chapter when we examine the richness of an "activist kitchen."

Veganism, like Love Activism, is non-hierarchical. This is because becoming vegan is a direct stance against *speciesism*. Speciesism assumes human superiority and places species on a hierarchical scale, which can then lead to conclusions that mistreating, using, and killing other species is okay. Similar to this, those who may subscribe to speciesist arguments

---

3 Thich Nhat Hanh, *How to Eat* (Berkeley, CA: Parallax Press, 2014), 59.

to condone violence against certain nonhuman animals, may think it is not okay to harm others, such as cats and dogs in the United States. Or, someone who loves and cares for horses may fight against using them as food, but sees no issue with eating other animals. Much of this is culturally-based, since clearly, for example, other cultures have no issue with using cats and dogs as food. Veganism completely disrupts these speciesist thoughts and advocates peace for all living beings.

Many people do not understand the difference between veganism and vegetarianism, so it is important to take a moment to explain exactly what veganism is. First, veganism within the context of ethics and activism is not just a diet for health reasons; it is truly a way of life. Vegans eat no animal products, but vegetarians may still consume eggs and dairy. Vegans do not purchase clothing made from animal skins and vegans do not use beauty and cleaning products that are tested on animals or made with animal ingredients. This is why it is incorrect to describe being vegan as just a diet. It is an essential practice toward living a kind and peaceful life that goes beyond food. It is a political statement.

Vegetarianism can be seen as a humane step toward a peaceful life, but vegetarianism still relies on the violence and suffering of the meat and dairy factory farming industries, which are known as well for their impact on climate change and environmental devastation.[4] I was a vegetarian for many years before becoming vegan and I now realize that I was complicit in the violence I thought I was taking a stand against, because of my continued consumption of cheese and dairy. Veganism is also not just against the killing of nonhuman animals, but also the use of them that is part of a cycle of abuse and cruelty. Vegetarians may purport to be against killing, I used to describe myself that way while vegetarian, but most vegetarian diets support violence, since the systems of factory farming where much of the industrialized world gets their food, including cheese, eggs, and dairy, are places of horror and deep sadness. Beyond this, it is very easy to find scientific evidence of the damage factory farming does to the natural world that contributes to global warming. To remove oneself as much as possible

---

4 Some studies of the impact on factory farming processes and environmental devastation, including global warming and climate change are the following: Gowri Koneswaran and Danielle Nierenberg, "Global Farm Animal Production and Global Warming: Impacting and Mitigating Climate Change," *Environmental Health Perspectives* 116, no. 5 (2008): 578-582, doi: 10.1289/ehp.11034; UN News Centre, "Rearing Cattle Produces More Greenhouse Gases than Driving Cars, UN Report Warns, Nov. 29, 2006, http://www.un.org/apps/news/story.asp?NewsID=20772#.WmLagDdG3IU; and "Factory Farming Takes Huge Toll on Human Health, Environment," CCPA Monitor 15, no. 3 (2008): 31.

from this violence, only veganism is advocated for within the context of Love Activism.

Just a decade ago the literature and advocacy for veganism was more limited. Today, however, if you are reading this and wish to discover the reasons for going vegan, a wealth of resources are available for you. To begin, you may watch some documentaries, such as *Earthlings*,[5] *Meet Your Meat*,[6] *Cowspiracy*,[7] and *Peaceable Kingdom: The Journey Home*.[8] Another excellent documentary of one man's journey to veganism is a freely available film titled, *The Witness*, by an organization called Tribe of Heart.[9] These films may contain content that disturbs and saddens you by its sheer violence, but it may help you to make a change in your life that will ultimately bring you much peace and joy by knowing you are rejecting such a devastating and violent system. A professor of food science I used to work with would require her students to tour a slaughterhouse as part of the class requirements. This was because she believed we must all be aware of where our food comes from and then make a personal and informed decision about eating animals after witnessing their killing.

You may also consider reading books about veganism, such as Will Tuttle's *The World Peace Diet: Eating for Spiritual Health and Social Harmony*;[10] A. Breeze Harper's *Sistah Vegan: Black Female Vegans Speak on Food, Identity, Health, and Society*;[11] or Brenda Davis and Vesanto Melina's *Becoming Vegan: The Complete Reference to Plant-Based Nutrition*.[12] There are many other books and cookbooks readily available at most bookstores

---

5 *Earthlings*, directed by Shaun Monson (2005; Burbank, CA: Earthlings.com, 2010), DVD. (*Earthlings* may be freely viewed at http://www.nationearth.com).

6 *Meet Your Meat*, directed by Bruce Friedrich (Norfolk, VA: PETA, 2002), DVD. (*Meet Your Meat* may be freely viewed at http://www.peta.org/videos/meet-your-meat).

7 *Cowspiracy*, directed by Kip Andersen and Keegan Kuhn (2014; San Rafael, CA: Earth Aware Editions, 2016), DVD.

8 *Peaceable Kingdom: The Journey Home*, directed by Jenny Stein (Australia: Tribe of Heart, 2012), DVD. (*Peaceable Kingdom* may be freely viewed at http://www.peaceablekingdomfilm.org).

9 *The Witness*, directed by Jenny Stein (2000, Ithaca, NY: Tribe of Heart, 2008), DVD. (*The Witness* may be freely viewed at http://www.witnessfilm.org/).

10 Will Tuttle, *The World Peace Diet: Eating for Spiritual Health and Social Harmony* (Brooklyn, NY: Lantern Books, 2004).

11 A. Breeze Harper, *Sistah Vegan: Black Female Vegans Speak on Food, Identity, Health, and Society* (Brooklyn, NY: Lantern Books, 2010).

12 Brenda Davis and Vesanto Melina, *Becoming Vegan: The Complete Reference to Plant-Based Nutrition* (Summertown, TN: Book Publishing Company, 2014).

and libraries that will help with preparing food.[13] You can also search a website called happycow.com to find vegan-friendly restaurants and markets in your area. If there is a Food Not Bombs group in your community, you may get involved with them to prepare and serve vegan meals to the poor and homeless. You may be surprised to discover that what you eat will expand once you become vegan, as if a whole world of new foods is revealed.

Beyond these possibilities, if you live near an animal sanctuary that advocates veganism, you may consider visiting the sanctuary. It is important to look for a sanctuary that includes farm animals, since they are more likely adhering to vegan ethics.[14] There may also be a vegan meet-up group in your community that can provide you support. Because eating is something we all do several times a day and it is often a social thing, you may experience confusion, ridicule, or even hostility from others who do not understand your decision. This may even occur with friends and family, which makes it important to have some sort of support system in place, whether virtually or in-person. As you begin your vegan journey, think of it as an exciting and experimental time in your life as an activist.

Your Activist Kitchen (And Home!)

Expanding on the theme of non-violence in our daily food choices, by practicing Love Activism you can make your entire home a place of non-violence and compassion. What a glorious thing it is to have a peaceful home. At the center of this you can create your activist kitchen. There are many things we can consider as elements of such a kitchen, including buying local produce and, if we have the space, growing our own food. Another consideration is how we clean our kitchen and home.

Instead of continuing to add to the throw-away culture, use organic cotton cloths over paper towels whenever possible. You can wash and use these cloths for years – even decades. When paper towels are necessary, use

---

13 The following are examples of vegan cookbooks: Isa Chandra Moskowitz, *Vegan with a Vengeance: Over 150 Delicious, Cheap, Animal-Free Recipes That Rock* (New York, NY: Marlowe & Company, 2005); Mike and Isy, *Another Dinner is Possible: More Than Just a Vegan Cookbook* (Oakland, CA: AK Press, 2007); and Bryant Terry, *Vegan Soul Kitchen: Fresh, Healthy, and Creative African-American Cuisine* (Cambridge, MA: Da Capo Press, 2009).

14 Examples of animal sanctuaries that advocate veganism are Farm Sanctuary (http://www.farmsanctuary.org/) with locations in Orland, California; Los Angeles, California; and Watkins Glen, New York and Leilani Farm Sanctuary in Maui, Hawaii (http://leilanifarmsanctuary.org/).

recycled and unbleached paper towels. (Recycled toilet paper and tissues are also available at many stores.)

In addition, instead of using products that may be toxic to the environment and your family, as well as containing animal ingredients, practice non-violence by making your own safe cleaning supplies. An effective and easy way to clean countertops, windows, mirrors, and some flooring is using a homemade mixture of water and vinegar. Vinegar is also a natural deterrent for ants and other insects. If you must purchase cleaning products, look for non-toxic and vegan cleaning supplies. There are so many companies making these products now. Remember that being labeled "cruelty-free" means the product was not tested on animals, but it does not automatically mean it is vegan, since "cruelty-free" products may still contain animal ingredients. Look for products that are specifically marked vegan or check the ingredients of "cruelty-free" ones, since they may be vegetarian and not vegan. (The same is true for cosmetics and bathing products.)

There are other intersecting issues with oppression in addition to violence and animal suffering that are essential to consider when purchasing goods and items for our homes. One of these issues surrounds the pay and treatment of the workers who grow and produce the food.

Non-violence requires buying fair trade and organic ingredients whenever possible as a statement for human rights and environmental protection. Organic is important, for example, not only for the environment, but for the workers who are otherwise exposed to harsh and disease-causing pesticides. Fair trade is important because it is a step toward knowing that the people involved with producing the food were given a fair wage. The fact that there are different fair trade labels can be confusing, but it is easy to discover the meanings behind them with a little research.[15] As you discover new companies and products, you may find yourself making a decision to start a personal boycott of companies you supported in the past. Products that are thought of as highly pleasurable, but can be the result of much suffering and exploitation include coffee, sugar, and chocolate. Thankfully, these are also products that are often available as fair trade goods at even major supermarkets. (Please see Lauren Ornelas' interview in the *Living Portraits: Interviews with Activists* section for more on issues with chocolate and food justice.)

---

15 There are several organizations that provide information on the different fair trade labels in the United States and beyond. One example is available here: https://www.oneworldfairtrade.net/pages/identifying-fair-trade

In addition to what you purchase for your activist kitchen, consider other ways you can support more compassionate living and stand up against violence throughout your home and in your daily life. How you shop for clothing and care for your clothing is one possibility. Instead of contributing to careless consumerism and supporting corporations that exploit garment workers in other countries, mend items. You can buy used clothing or learn how to make your own. You can wear things until they need to be replaced for wear and tear and not because of a change dictated by the media and fashion industry. Besides, your fashion statement will be one of compassion, activism, and human rights, not materialism and trends. If you are buying clothes, look for organic and fair trade whenever possible through online organizations or, if you are fortunate, a store in your area. Accessories, such as earrings and scarves, can often be found as fair trade. The same is true for art and other decorations for your home, which you may also buy direct from artists at arts and crafts fairs. By purchasing this way, you help to ensure that the people who created what you are going to wear or display as a thing of beauty in your home were paid a more fair and just wage. If you cannot determine if something is fair trade, ask the store who made it and where it is from. Shouldn't they know? Shouldn't we all know?

Practices of Non-Violence: go vegan; reject racist jokes; buy fair trade clothing, coffee, and other goods; boycott companies that profit from violence; stand up to bullies; speak out against war; buy organic food; buy cruelty free cosmetics and cleaning supplies; capture and release insects...

Self-Care

Colors: earth, terracotta, clay, raw sienna

Self-care makes us strong and better able to care for others. There is nothing selfish about taking time and energy to do things for ourselves that will ultimately result in bringing more joy to those we interact with. When we are physically and emotionally healthy, we can offer more love to others. Mindfulness educator Mare Chapman writes that, "because everything is truly interdependent and nothing and no one exists completely independently…" we should see working on ourselves as "responsible, wise, and kind, rather than selfish."[1] A popular and powerful quote on self-care that rises out of the cruel realities of racism and homophobia comes from the black lesbian poet and activist Audre Lorde: "Caring for myself is not self-indulgence, it is self-preservation, and that is an act of political warfare."[2] Activists who do not practice self-care can easily experience burn-out and despair under the weight of all they are fighting to eradicate. Here we will examine a few possibilities for caring for ourselves, so that we may build strong foundations and sharpen our resilience.

Body Love

If there is a woman in our society who has not struggled with a difficult relationship with food, I haven't met her. If there is a woman in our

---

1 Mare Chapman, *Unshakeable Confidence: The Freedom to Be Our Authentic Selves* (Madison, WI: Mare Chapman, LLC, 2017), 4.

2 Audre Lorde, *A Burst of Light: Essays* (Ithaca, NY: Firebrand Books, 1988), 131.

society who does not currently or hasn't at some point in her life struggled with her body image, I haven't met her either. It seems that these things often go together. Even women who seem confident, like they hold the world in the palms of their hands, have told me about their difficulties with food and body.

When I first heard about how women's images were digitally altered for advertisements, fashion magazines, and other media, which is many years ago when I was a young girl, I was shocked. It was later that I also discovered the practice of using parts from different women to manufacture a cover model, meaning that the woman we see on the cover is sometimes composed of one woman's eyes, another woman's hair, and so on. When I considered this, I thought, how can we ever win? There is nothing realistic in these images. Magazines, billboards, and various media intrusions show us "acceptable," often ultra-thin, and white bodies that reflect only a small percentage of real women's bodies. Clarissa Pinkola Estes, in *The Joyous Body*,[3] places these images in what she calls the "overculture," which moves us away from our true essence and celebrating ourselves as we are.

One way for women to perform self-care is to reject these harmful images and work at accepting ourselves through body-positive practices that we individually discover are best for our unique needs. It may be a lifelong and courageous journey to reach a positive relationship with our bodies. Returning to Estes' work in *The Joyous Body*, which is recommended for anyone wishing to move from judging to loving your body, she presents the body as a magnificent and loyal "consort," meaning it is a grand and special companion we have throughout our lives. She also uses the helpful metaphor of trees as human bodies. This includes the need for a strong root system to withstand storms; being nourished through our wounds; learning compassion and mercy through illness; and recognizing scars as beautiful marks that tell the stories of our lives, including possibly withstanding great difficulties and surviving. An aging body is also celebrated as something to not hide, but to recognize for its wisdom and longevity. Like an older tree, the aging body has been tested and is able to sway with confidence in the wind, since it has already witnessed and lived through many storms. In *The Earth Path*, Starhawk, also using trees as metaphors for bodies, beautifully writes, "Like redwoods, as we get older

---

3 Clarissa Pinkola Estes, *The Joyous Body: Myths & Stories of the Wise Woman Archetype*, Sounds True, 2011, compact disc.

we get thicker."[4] This conjures up a magnificent image that works against the compulsive and destructive practices and beliefs brought on by a fat-phobic culture.

As you begin your journey toward body love, I recommend you find representations of bodies in art or other places that represent your truth. When you are faced with images from the "overculture" that conflict with your truth and beauty, you can look at or remember these other representations you have found. You may decide to place them at a home altar, near a mirror you use when getting ready for work or school, or on a vision board. I have done this before with images of ancient art from difficult cultures that were created in reverence to the goddess or Great Mother. I first encountered these representations as a young woman at the Los Angeles County Museum of Art. I was not looking for them, but came upon a collection of goddess figurines by chance. Once I found myself in front of them, I stayed for a long time. I was absolutely mesmerized. As this occurred, I did not process why I was so struck by the figurines, but later I reflected on how I saw myself in some of them. Eventually I discovered the work of Marija Gimbutas, particularly *The Language of the Goddess*,[5] which provides illustrations of artifacts and figurines created with goddess imagery. How affirming these images can be, as they not only show aspects of real women's bodies we rarely see, such as rounder stomachs, and heavy and hanging breasts, but they are objects of reverence.

All of us need to find diverse representatives of strong women to celebrate, including women that look like us or our family members, as well as women leading lives that may inspire us or provide examples of different ways we can lead our lives. This is important for all genders, but especially so for girls and young women. There is too much of a single narrative of a woman held up as an oppressive ideal and we all know what she looks like. She is usually of a middle or upper economic class. She is typically with a husband and children, white, thin, and spending a good amount of her time conforming and reinforcing images of "beauty" and "success." This single image hurts all of us. It enforces white supremacy. It also advocates for a specific lifestyle, which can restrict freedom and cause us to put off following our true dreams and callings for years or possibly forever. For a young person, it validates just one path that is admired and sure to bring love and happiness, which we all know is not correct.

---

4 Starhawk, *The Earth Path*, 120.

5 Marija Gimbutas, *The Language of the Goddess* (New York, NY: Thames & Hudson, 1989).

In addition to finding representative and diverse images, there are body-positive organizations that provide courses and free information. A great example is Be Nourished, which is based in Portland, Oregon. The founders, Hilary Kinavey and Dana Sturtevant, are concerned about the intersection of health, food, weight, and body image. The organization "is founded on the idea that we are all born with remarkable instincts to love and care for our bodies."[6] The Be Nourished Manifesto available on the organization's website is definitely worth a read. This is just one resource you may find helpful. Thankfully, there are many others out there that are doing this positive work. You may also consider reading memoirs that examine these issues, since knowing you are not alone is incredibly helpful. Roxane Gay's *Hunger: A Memoir of (My) Body*[7] is a powerful story of trauma, weight, and body image. Lucy Grealy's *Autobiography of a Face*[8] is a stunning personal narrative of the restrictive definition of "beauty" and the cruelty she experienced due to disfigurement from cancer.

Moving beyond the concept of "body love," diverse representations of strong women can also provide something I think of as an interior sustenance. What I mean by this is that seeking out different life narratives can also be a great practice of self-care by demonstrating how much *within* us is important, since the "over-culture" puts such an emphasis on our outward appearance at the expense of the richness we have inside. As an older woman, I can look back on my life and realize that through all the oppressive, single narratives there were many women in the punk rock scene, and specifically two women I saw as a young woman in college, that showed a different path. One example was June Jordan, who I mentioned earlier in this book. Jordan presented the life of an activist and poet as something noble and important. In her class, "Coming into the World Female," at UC Berkeley in 1993, we mostly read poetry and I further discovered the important intersection of truth, art, and activism.

There was another English professor I had who influenced me when I encountered her on the street for a moment that lasted less than five minutes. She would have no idea of this impact. What I saw in her was a woman living a joyful life of the mind who was not concerned with wearing the latest style of clothing. One could say her hair was wild or "messy" and her

---

6 Read about the mission of Be Nourished at http://benourished.org/about

7 Roxane Gay, *Hunger: A Memoir of (My) Body* (New York, NY: HarperCollins, 2017).

8 Lucy Grealy, *Autobiography of a Face* (Boston, MA: Harper Perennial, 1994).

entire appearance stood in stark contrast to conventional images of beauty. When I encountered her carrying a bag of groceries on a Berkeley sidewalk, I imagine she was in her 50s or 60s and I would have been around twenty-two. She recognized me as a student in her class. We shared a brief greeting and this tiny glimpse into her life was profound. Obviously, this is within the privileged context of UC Berkeley, but it opened up possibilities for me that I had not considered. Over the years after this, when I worked at soulless, horrible jobs, I kept magic in my life by not giving up my love of books and writing. I longed for the evenings and weekends when I could envelope myself in this life of the mind, which gave me that interior sustenance I mentioned above. Jordan and this other English professor showed me how much more was available in life beyond the restrictive, traditional narrative. Look for women like these in your community, if you haven't already found them. I assure you they are around you.

Imposter Phenomenon

Beyond body image issues discussed above that can impact our wellbeing and potentially make us question our worth, we may at times question our intellect, which can lead to self-esteem issues and even negatively impact the far-reaching potential we have as activists. I know I have missed out on opportunities in my life and have been afraid to speak up at times, so I am writing this section in order to help anyone reading who shares these harmful and limiting feelings.

As a community college student, my dream was to transfer to UC Berkeley. I knew of its history of student activism and overall prestige as a university and somehow I started to think I could get in. I worked full-time and attended the community college full-time, but still managed to do very well, even though I was continuing to go to punk shows and stay out late. I remember even taking books to read on the dirty floors at different clubs! I truly gave it my all and felt I was starting to make a new and different future for myself, so it deeply hurt when an academic counselor discouraged me from even applying. I am not sure why this person did not believe in me, but thankfully my punk rock youth made me want to fight, so I independently researched the transfer requirements and when the time came I applied to Berkeley and was accepted.

When I transferred from the community college to Berkeley, I was very excited to discover there were many libraries on campus. When I first ventured into the Doe Library, the main library on campus, I could not believe the beauty and grandeur. I used the online catalog, which was still in a primitive state at that time, to search for books. With some call numbers jotted down, I set out to find them. Around and around I went trying to find the books I wanted to no avail. I was embarrassed to ask someone for help, so I kept trying to find them on my own. After doing this for a long time, I got up the courage to ask a library staff member for help.

While at Berkeley, a fear came over me at different times. The fear had to do with my professors, university staff members, and sometimes other students discovering that I did not belong there. I felt that I had to work hard to conceal that I was not really smart enough or cultured enough. I was even afraid that the way I spoke, possibly using slang or incorrect grammar, might reveal something. I read every page assigned with as much focus as possible, since I believed I could not afford even a tiny slip.

This fear of being "found out" did not stop after graduating from Berkeley. What an accomplishment that was, but then I found myself in graduate school and the same fears reappeared. I imagined other students saw me as from a lower class. One of the worst examples was when I had to sit in front of a panel of three professors for the oral comprehensive exam for my first master's degree. This is a frightening experience for most people. I had the extra fear of thinking I was going to finally be "found out." No longer would I be able to hide the fact that I wasn't really that smart. Now they would know that I managed to make it through only with my inherited endurance and grit.

Now that I am much older and I have shared these experiences with colleagues, students, and friends, I have discovered that many others have such fears. Like so many difficult things in life, when we are in the midst of them, we are afraid to tell anyone and we feel alone in our struggle. In my situation, I believe it was because my parents did not go to college and many of the people I encountered were from an upper economic class. They were groomed for the university, but I saw myself as a lucky outsider who was barely hanging on. There is some truth to my story, since I did need to often scramble to get caught up on theories or authors I was not familiar with, but it didn't mean I didn't belong there. Several years ago while searching in a psychology database for articles I came across something called the Imposter Phenomenon (IP). This is exactly what I had experienced. I believed I was an imposter in the academic world. I can't say I am completely immune to this phenomenon, but now that I am older I just care less about what people think of me and how "cultured" I appear. How freeing this is. I like sharing this story with students at the community college where I work. Hopefully it will help some of them who are planning to transfer to a university.

Why am I mentioning IP here in this chapter on self-care? It is because this notion of not being good enough is something so many of us suffer with alone. It can impede our ability to do things we believe in and cause us a great amount of stress. It may even impact the extent of our activism. A study of college students by Loretta Neal McGregor, Damon E. Gee, and K. Elizabeth Posey found that "individuals who feel like an imposter may not achieve as much as they are capable of because depressive symptoms may impede their productivity."[9] Similarly, Joel Lane's study of adults transitioning from college to professional life reports that suffering from "IP poses a significant threat to well-being."[10] Individuals may minimize their achievements and attribute "accomplishments to luck, good fortune, or some other external cause."[11] Rosalyn Lang, an African-American woman featured in Susan Pinker's *Psychology Today* article, is one such example. Although Lang has achieved much success, including a Ph.D. in molecular biology, "she felt undeserving, attributing any triumphs to luck, affirmative action, and sheer elbow grease."[12] The article on Lang reports that 93% of African-American female college students suffer from aspects of IP, a phenomenon "linked to perfectionism, burnout, and depression."[13] Racism; gender and class stereotypes; and discriminatory views towards those with disabilities are all factors that create and reinforce IP.

Knowing about IP, what can we do to work against it for ourselves and others? Safe support systems are one possibility, including friends that we can share and discuss IP thoughts with. Moving away and protecting ourselves from individuals who reinforce IP, if possible, is another strategy. Receiving help from a therapist or psychologist is another possibility. Try not to compare yourself to others, but move forward with your own work. Make a list of your accomplishments that you can look at when

---

9 Loretta Neal McGregor, Damon E. Gee, and K. Elizabeth Posey, "I Feel Like a Fraud and It Depresses Me: The Relation between the Imposter Phenomenon and Depression," *Social Behavior and Personality* 36, no. 1 (2008): 47.

10 Joel A. Lane, "The Imposter Phenomenon among Emerging Adults Transitioning into Professional Life: Developing a Grounded Theory," *Adultspan Journal* 14, no. 2 (2015): 115.

11 Lane, 120.

12 Susan Pinker, "Extra Credit: Some True Successes Say Their Laurels are Unearned," *Psychology Today*, Nov/Dec 2009, 39.

13 Pinker, 39.

you doubt yourself. Now that IP is discussed quite a bit, an Internet search for "imposter phenomenon" or "imposter syndrome" will bring back various articles and quizzes meant to help, which you can research on your own to determine their value. Consider how making yourself stronger is a form of personal activism that will potentially allow you to do more to impact the world.

Peaceful Viewing

What we spend our time with and allow into our minds and bodies can also contribute to how well we care for ourselves. Queen Afua's *Sacred Woman* provides wise advice in this realm. One section is on the issue of consumption with an understanding of consumption that includes what we see and hear and not just what we eat. "We must also be aware of the television programming we consume," she states, "for what we watch creates who we become."[14] She specifically makes note of "constant violence, blind consumerism, and fear." This is similar to "The Fifth Mindfulness Training: Nourishment and Healing" from Deerpark Monastery's *Mindfulness Trainings Recitation Booklet*, which points to the suffering caused by consuming materials with "toxins," including certain media.[15] Practicing self-care may require an examination of what we are consuming beyond food and then considering how these things may negatively impact how we feel about ourselves and others, ultimately causing a potential block in our growth as love activists.

Like most of us, I've experienced being compelled to watch a particular television show or film that is full of shock value with little substance. Or, perhaps there was some substance and incredibly smart writing and good acting, so I was drawn in to what turned out to be a sad and tragic pit. On other occasions, especially with "reality" shows, competition, nasty behavior, and superficiality reigned while I sat and watched as if under a spell. Before I knew it, hours were wasted.

I came to associate a lot of this television programming with what I believe is our culture of meanness or bully culture. Trying to win at any cost and making fun of others is what these types of shows force onto

---

14 Queen Afua, *Sacred Woman: A Guide to Healing the Feminine Body, Mind, and Spirit* (New York, NY: One World, 2000), 164.

15 Deer Park Monastery, *Mindfulness Trainings Recitation Booklet*, 17

us. Teddy Wayne's article, "The Culture of Nastiness", gets to the essence of this. "In the dog-eat-dog environments of these programs, cooperation and kindness are readily abandoned for back-stabbing and character assassination,"[16] he writes. Why would someone sacrifice for another, Wayne asks, if only one person can win. He uses the "Real Housewives" series as another example of how "calm conflict resolution does not make for good ratings,"[17] but fighting and being cruel certainly does. How popular this form of "entertainment" has become is truly disheartening.

It was so troubling and deeply sad to watch the 2016 United States presidential election. Name-calling and bullying had finally reached the largest stage. Instead of rejecting it, many people laughed along, embraced it, or let it pass. Of course, politics has always been a ruthless and corrupt business, but now we were seeing something else. The culture of meanness or bully culture of reality television received a halo. At times I watched political rallies and heard large crowds laughing when someone was ridiculed, mimicked, or called a nasty name. People unfortunately saw strength in this and even thought it was okay to not apologize. Since the election, I have heard similar comments countless times, such as, "Get over it. You lost" or, "They are just poor losers and cry babies. We won!" A presidential election, though, is not a reality show or a football game. These comments show how much this thinking is embedded in our culture.

Another issue with a lot of "reality" programming is that it presents a "norm" that many of us do not fit into. This can cause an alienating feeling. For several months I became fascinated with house hunting and renovation shows. The storylines were almost always the same. There was a couple and they needed a lot of space and many bathrooms. They acted like things were easily at their disposal. In fact, they usually were. Most got the houses they wanted and the plethora of problems they encountered were worked out. When extra money was needed, they appeared stressed, but ultimately the money was almost always found. If we think about most people from low to lower-middle economic classes, this is far from "reality." How does watching these shows help us to care for ourselves and be love activists? Whose stories and whose reality is being portrayed?

When it comes to viewing media, I decided to start asking myself two questions: "How do I feel after watching that?" and "Does watching this make me want to love more?" If I felt empty, depressed, or anxious,

---

16 Teddy Wayne, "The Culture of Nastiness," *New York Times*, Feb. 19, 2017, 2.

17 Wayne, 2.

clearly I was not nourishing my soul, so I decided to resist. It can be hard to not watch some of this programming though. It can be as addictive as fast food and so easy to access. Truly, though, our lives pass by so quickly. It is disheartening to know that many people work at unsatisfying jobs to only come home to watch something thought of as "an escape." Aren't there profoundly better ways to escape? And shouldn't we even examine this unfortunate need to escape from our lives? Why waste our time when there is so much we could be doing for ourselves and others to make the world more beautiful. Take good care of yourself. Consume things that heal and nourish you. You are worth it and the world needs you.

Practices Of Self-Care: talk with a therapist or spiritual advisor; rest when you are tired; ride a bike; take walks; love and accept your body; forgive yourself, remembering that we all make mistakes; ask for help/tell a friend when you are suffering; take a bubble bath; find body-positive resources; reject media that does not heal and nourish your soul...

Creativity

Colors: red, maroon, hint of gold

Creativity as an element of Love Activism happens when we ourselves create art, when we support the art of others, and also when we bring our creative knowledge as gifts to the community through teaching. In *Women Who Run with the Wolves*, Clarissa Pinkola Estes provides a beautiful quote on the power of creativity: "Creativity is not a solitary movement. That is its power. Whatever is touched by it, whoever hears it, sees it, senses it, knows it, is fed…. A single creative act has the potential to feed a continent."[1]

I love Estes' idea of feeding a continent. Isn't it also true that some creative acts have the ability to feed across generations? It is not hard to think of certain works, which may be paintings, songs, poems, novels, or other representations from the art world, that are beloved by all ages of people from very different walks of life. As activists, we can use our creativity, which takes courage, to bring works into the world that may add beauty, represent freedom of expression, and/or illustrate a social or political statement.

Do not feel that taking time for artmaking moves you away from activism. In "Making Art During Fascism," Beth Pickens provides the wise statement that "art helps other people process the times we are in and live their lives."[2] She also comments on the positive results of artmaking for artists, alluding to its relation to self-care and self-preservation.

1 Clarissa Pinkola Estes, *Women Who Run with the Wolves* (New York, NY: Ballantine Books, 1992), 298.

2 Beth Pickens, *Making Art During Fascism v. 2.0* (Los Angeles, CA: Women's Center for Creative Work, Feb. 2017), 11, zine.

Art therapist Shaun McNiff, who believes "art and creativity are the soul's medicine,"[3] also points out how angry and revolutionary works "that aggressively provoke audiences and decry the conditions of the world can embody important aspects of the healing process where the identification and destruction of harmful patterns is necessary."[4] Ultimately, art is an avenue for sustaining, informing, healing, inspiring, and expressing, which are all very necessary for the creator and the audience.

Roadblocks to Creativity

Finding time is one of the major roadblocks to creating. It often feels like work and other responsibilities take all of our energy. Even when we have a desire to create, we can feel too tired or not have the necessary solitude and space. Like with all things though, if the desire burns within you to create, try and find even tiny pockets where you can. If you think about your day, hopefully you find you do have a little time you can piece together.

I recently read an article about a woman who published her first novel at age forty-seven.[5] It wasn't easy. She sometimes wrote in her car on a laptop while waiting for her children at appointments. This story reminded me of the time I saw the writer Susan Straight speak at a conference. Straight talked about getting in her car to get away from her noisy home and ultimately writing a book in a Ralphs Grocery Store parking lot. I have spent countless lunch hours writing and reading. Sometimes it was only that lunch hour when I had breathing space and quiet time. One of my former co-workers joked with me that I read more books on my lunch hour than most people read in a lifetime. There was a time when I worked one full-time job and two part-time jobs to make ends meet. Somehow I managed to write my first book within the midst of that craziness. One thing I did was remove as many non-essential distractions from my life, such as television, and I would write whenever I could, even in chaotic laundromats.

Another roadblock to creativity is the need to feel in control. Artmaking requires that you allow yourself to venture into unknown territory and to not be afraid. One of the best books I have read on creativity,

---

3 Shaun McNiff, *Art Heals: How Creativity Cures the Soul* (Boulder, CO: Shambhala, 2004), xii-xiii.

4 McNiff, 6-7.

5 Robin Finn, "Time to Let Go and Pursue a Dream," *Los Angeles Times*, Mar. 4, 2017, F6.

although it never mentions that word in the book, is, *Art & Fear: Observations on the Perils (and Rewards) of Artmaking*, by David Bayles and Ted Orland. They write, "People who need certainty in their lives are less likely to make art that is risky, subversive, complicated, iffy, suggestive or spontaneous.... Uncertainty is the essential, inevitable and all-pervasive companion to your desire to make art."[6] Do not let a fear of experimentation, mistakes, or what others may think prevent you from creating. It is important to also remember that there is definitely a degree of subjectivity when it comes to viewing art. We have all experienced that gut reaction when we see something that speaks directly to us or repels us. Considering this, even if we were to create a work that many people would call a masterpiece, we could surely find people who feel no connection to the creation and may even abhor it. Do not worry about the audience. Just create and move forward.

Letting Go of Expertise and Perfection/Embracing DIY Ethics

The notions of expertise and perfection are also roadblocks to creativity, but they are so ingrained in our culture that they deserve their own section here. At UC Berkeley and in the community, June Jordan taught a class titled, "Poetry for the People." Poetry was not something for the privileged and elite who wrote and spoke in a certain way. Poetry was for everyone. Within this vision is the idea that all of us can be poets. I firmly believe this. Sometimes it may just take some encouragement.

Jordan's belief is how I feel about all art forms. We all have the ability within us to be artists. We do not need advanced and specialized education. These beliefs are similar to the DIY or do-it-yourself culture I was immersed in within the punk rock scene of the 1980s. We did not need permission from record companies, publishers, or some other form of authority to create. Anyone could pick up an instrument and anyone could self-publish. During this time, I worked on a zine with my friends titled, *Anti-Establishment*. We were teenagers with no real experience to create a magazine, but we wrote articles and interviewed bands. We then pasted our creations on paper in a collage style and photocopied and stapled the pages together. We sold our zine at record and punk rock stores and mailed it around the U.S. and sometimes to people in other countries. We didn't need to be experts to create.

---

6 David Bayles and Ted Orland, *Art & Fear: Observations on the Perils (and Rewards) of Artmaking* (Santa Cruz, CA: Image Continuum, 1993), 21.

Sometimes, as we get older, a fear of creating appears in our lives. Letting go of the notion of expertise can help with this. I have a couple examples.

A few years ago I decided to take guitar lessons. I was around age forty-four. I believe when I started I wanted to master the instrument to a certain extent, but it turned out to be much more difficult than I anticipated, which could be due to my age, talent, or a combination of both. Around the time I discovered this, though, I was also having so much fun with my lessons and the few chords my fingers could handle. I certainly could not keep time and changing between chords was incredibly clumsy and slow (it still is!). What happened is that I started to write my own songs. Within a few months, I had several songs. Singing and playing these songs, though incredibly messy at times, brought me great joy. I considered that if I practiced the guitar for a good amount of time each day and really worked at it that I may get to a place where my songs would be okay and I could possibly play with other beginners, but with my work schedule, writing, and doing so many other things that were important to me, I was honest with myself that I did not need to become more accomplished. The little I got from the lessons and the great teacher I already had gave me what I wanted, since I always had a desire to play music. I still sing and play one of my songs often and will sometimes just sit and strum the guitar.

A similar thing occurred when I recently took a ceramics class. Like the guitar, it was something I always had a desire to do. In my ceramics class there were people with varied experience. The class was almost like an open studio, so some of the people with a lot of experience created vases and other objects while a few people, like me, were learning things for the first time. I discovered that I enjoyed making pendants with words and other hand built pieces that also had lettering or words as part of the design (Fig 3). I admired the work of others, particularly graceful pieces made on the potter's wheel, but I worked at not comparing what I was making to their creations. The experience of creating and being in that environment was more important. The class was truly exhilarating. These experiences with the guitar and ceramics have taught me a great deal about creativity and letting go of fear and expertise, which gets to my next point about teaching others.

There are other things I just started to do on my own after age forty without any education, including painting and making mixed media works. Although I made collages most of my life, I never incorporated painting with the process. Many of the pieces I make are also related to Love Activism, since I add text with messages related to feminism, peace, self-care, and other issues. By embracing DIY ethics and not worrying about what others think during the creative process, I have gone beyond

Fig 3

creating my own mixed media works to providing workshops for others, including foster youth and college students in my community. In addition to providing the supplies for them to create their own art, I discuss DIY culture with them and the ideas of letting go of expertise and fear.

When you think about your life, is there a form of artmaking you could teach others, whether or not you believe you are a master? Is there something you have always wanted to learn? Is there a way you can combine your creativity with your activism? If you feel you need more confidence before exploring, one possibility is to research outsider art or self-taught artists to see all the wonders that other people have created. A good resource for outsider art is *Raw Vision* magazine,[7] as well as some books and galleries[8] that showcase self-taught artists that are often living and creating outside of the art establishment.

---

7 Visit http://rawvision.com to discover more about Raw Vision magazine. *An Outsider Art Sourcebook* is available for purchase and download from the website. The sourcebook features biographies of nearly 200 artists, along with images of their creative work.

8 Betty-Carol Sellen's book *Self-Taught, Outsider and Folk Art* (3rd edition, 2016, McFarland & Company, Jefferson, North Carolina) and John Maizels' *Raw Creation: Outsider Art and Beyond* (2015, Phaidon, London, England) are two book resources for discovering outsider art. Many museums and galleries around the world feature self-taught artists, including Intuit: The Center for Intuitive and Outsider Art in Chicago, Illinois (http://www.art.org) and the American Visionary Art Museum in Baltimore, Maryland (http://www.avam.org).

Craftivism

An amazing example of using creativity as part of one's activism can be found in the work of craftivists who make art for the greater good. Some large scale examples that can fall under the realm of craftivism are the AIDS Memorial Quilt and the knitted pink pussy hats that many protesters used during the Global Women's March in 2017. Betsy Greer coined the term craftivism in 2002. In *Craftivism: The Art of Craft and Activism*, she states, "I felt that artists needed a term for crafting that was motivated by social or political activism, and 'craftivism' fit the bill."[9] Throughout Greer's book there are various examples of craft as activism, including using quilting, cross-stitching, knitting, sewing, and ceramics. In one inspiring essay, Sayraphim Lothian discusses her concept of "Guerrilla Kindness," which involves placing her small handcrafted art pieces around different cities for people to find. "I practice random acts of guerrilla kindness to lift people's moods and make them happy,"[10] she explains. Another example of craftivism is in the collaborative work of Terrilynn's "The Uterus Flag Project." For this fiber arts project, individuals contribute their unique piece by stitching over an image of a uterus. Terrilynn explains that her "mission is to educate through the power of art that integrates the ideals of feminism, to change consciousness about women's health, and to include craftivism as an alternative way of giving voice to women."[11] "The Uterus Flag Project" also illustrates the collaboration that sometimes occurs with craftivism, which is one of its positive aspects as a community-building activism.

The Craftivist Collective, founded by Sarah Corbett in 2009, provides another example of collaboration. Corbett, an activist for many years was "feeling discouraged and exhausted"[12] when she started cross-stitching and realized how she could use her craft as a form of activism. In *A Little Book of Craftivism* she provides stunning examples, including mini cross-stitched banners hung in public places with thought-provoking messages of protest. She provides an idea for individuals to work together by creating unique small patches with protest statements that are then stitched together to

---

9 Betsy Greer, *Craftivism: The Art of Craft and Activism* (Vancouver, BC: Arsenal Pulp Press, 2014), 8.

10 Sayraphim Lothian, "Guerrilla Kindness," in *Craftivism: The Art of Craft and Activism*, ed. Betsy Greer (Vancouver, BC: Arsenal Pulp Press, 2014), 11.

11 Terrilynn, "The Uterus Flag Project," in *Craftivism: The Art of Craft and Activism*, ed. Betsy Greer (Vancouver, BC: Arsenal Pulp Press, 2014), 201.

12 Corbett, *A Little Book of Craftivism*, 3.

create a large quilt. The collective she started now has thousands of members throughout the world performing activism through various forms of crafting.

Zines

Zines are an excellent example of a creative form of expression that is accessible to all of us. Above I mentioned zines within the discussion of DIY. Considering that I was creating zines with my friends as teenagers, you can see how it is such an open and easy process in many respects. After first creating zines in the 1980s and early 1990s, I got busy with life and other projects before returning to zines a few years ago. Since I associated them with punk rock and a relatively small underground music movement, I was completely surprised and elated when I discovered that zine culture is larger now than ever and has expanded into other areas that may have little or nothing to do with punk rock. A zine can truly be about anything. It shows how the evolution of a vibrant art form takes place. (Fig. 4 provides an examples of different zines.)

Creating a zine is a way for you to express yourself without the need of any filter or authority, such as a publisher. The content of some zines is specifically political and about social justice issues. There are also many zines that focus on animal rights and veganism. Other zines may be more literary

Fig 4

in nature, such as a poetry zine. Art zines and collage zines are another form that may have pages full of illustrations. Another type to mention that can also be a great avenue for activist work is the personal zine, which is a genre called perzines. A perzine could be in the form of an autobiography. Some perzines are also related to self-care. Ultimately, zines can help you share a political, artistic, or personal message you wish to get out into the world.

There are different ways to create a zine. You can simply use a booklet template in a word processing program. You can also just get pieces of paper and glue images or text onto the page and then make photocopies to assemble your zine. Although many zines come in a booklet format, some people get very creative and make the zine a unique work of art. A quick search of zines online will reveal all of the possibilities.

Zines are such a major part of art and literary culture now that some libraries even have zine collections.[13] In addition, there are festivals that take place on an annual basis, some quite large and free to attend, that feature up to hundreds of zinesters showcasing their work for purchase or trade.[14] At these festivals, known as zine fests, there are also often workshops, including some that provide instruction and hands-on zine creation. You can also find zines for sale online, including places like etsy or through small, independent publishers. The popularity of zines has resulted in some publications about them, such as Alex Wrekk's *Stolen Sharpie Revolution: A DIY Resource for Zines and Zine Culture*.[15]

Supporting Others

One thing zine fests do so well is build community, which is something needed for all art forms. To sustain a strong creative community, it is essential to support each other. It was in Carolyn See's magical book, *Making a Literary Life*,[16] that I first encountered an idea that seems so obvious,

---

13 Visit the Barnard College page on zine libraries to discover libraries in the United States and beyond: https://zines.barnard.edu/zine-libraries

14 Visit the Stolen Sharpie Revolution website event page for a global list of zine fests: http://www.stolensharpierevolution.org/events/

15 Alex Wrekk, *Stolen Sharpie Revolution: A DIY Resource for Zines and Zine Culture* (Portland, OR: Lunchroom Publishing, 2009).

16 Carolyn See, *Making a Literary Life: Advice for Writers and Other Dreamers* (New York: NY: Random House, 2002), 37-47.

but could be done much more, which is simply reaching out to people to tell them you love what they create. See calls these "charming notes." You never know what kind of day someone is having. An individual you imagine as successful and not in need of a compliment may actually be struggling with depression or loneliness. Reviews can be hostile and social media comments cruel to even beloved artists, so letting someone know you recognize their courage and like what they are creating is a positive way to balance this out. Your kind "thank you" note with words of appreciation for the article, zine, book, painting, song, or other work may arrive at just the right time.

Other ways to support people's creativity involves taking the time to attend events and, of course, purchasing their work or making a donation, if you are able. Imagine the creator is holding an event of some kind in a gallery, bookstore, or other venue to share a work that possibly took months or years to create and no one comes to take part in the celebration. Your time, presence, and funding shows the importance of creativity for the community. Indeed, your support is love in action.

Practices of Creativity: teach someone how to paint or play an instrument; write poetry; collage; make handmade cards for your friends; visit a museum; see an independent film; donate to an art organization; take an art class; cook/bake; support local artists; send a "thank you" note to a writer, poet, or artist you admire; read about self-taught artists; support community radio stations that feature local artists; create a zine...

Feminism

Colors: lilac, pink rose

Feminism happens when we do not place gender restrictions on others; when we embrace equality, when we allow all humans, regardless of gender, to reach their full potential; when we don't make assumptions based on gender; and when we speak out against violence against women. Because all genders suffer when one is oppressed, embracing feminism and becoming an ally of feminists, regardless of one's gender, is a step toward liberation for all of us.

Let's first consider a few personal examples and beyond:

- Globally, 1 in 3 women are estimated to suffer physical and/or sexual intimate partner violence or sexual violence from a non-partner in their lifetime. Most of the violence is from an intimate partner. On a global scale, 38% of women murdered were killed by a male intimate partner.[1]

- Once at an old workplace of mine we received news that a female client had been raped outside of her apartment complex. It happened late in the evening when she was returning from somewhere and was walking from where she parked her car to her front door. A female co-worker, upon hearing this news, said out loud, "What was she doing out so late?"

- In the United States, 1 in 6 women has been the victim of attempted or completed rape during her lifetime. 90% of adult rape victims are

---

1 World Health Organization, "Violence against Women: Intimate Partner and Sexual Violence against Women Fact Sheet," *World Health Organization*, Nov. 2017, http://www.who.int/mediacentre/factsheets/fs239/en/

female. 13% of women who are raped attempt suicide and 33% contemplate ending their lives.[2]

- Victims of honor killings and honor violence are often women who are said to have brought shame on their family. Nearly 1,100 women were killed in honor-related attacks in Pakistan in 2015, according to the country's independent Human Rights Commission. Most of the women were shot, but attacks with acid were also common. Exercising a right to choose their partner in marriage, alleged illicit behavior, and other domestic disputes were the predominant causes given for the women losing their lives. Nearly 800 women during the same year committed or attempted suicide.[3]

- In *We Should All Be Feminists* Chimamanda Ngozi Adichie recalls, "I know a Nigerian woman who decided to sell her house because she didn't want to intimidate a man who might want to marry her."[4]

- As a young community college student, I was trying to get a seat in an impacted math class. I desperately wanted this class, since I would face putting off my graduation for an additional semester without it. The professor said he would only accept one more student. Four or five male students also wanted this seat. We were instructed to write a paragraph on why we should be the one allowed in the class. I wrote my heart out, explaining my intent to transfer and that I was a hard-working and dedicated student. The professor sat in his office and read each of our statements while we waited outside in the hallway. He came out and said, "Stacy gets the seat." I was elated. As we walked away, the guys were grumbling and one of them said, "Of course you would get it, because you are a girl."

- At my community reading group, one woman shared that she purposely selected her small apartment, because she could see into all the rooms when she came in the front door and it would be easy to find if someone was hiding inside. As the discussion continued, all of the women shared that they have experienced checking through their homes at different

---

2 Rape, Abuse and Incest National Network, "Victims of Sexual Violence: Statistics," *RAINN*, 2018, https://www.rainn.org/statistics/victims-sexual-violence

3 "Pakistan Honour Killings on the Rise, Report Reveals," *BBC News*, April 1, 2016, http://www.bbc.com/news/world-asia-35943732

4 Adichie, *We Should All Be Feminists*, 29.

times in their lives, even looking in closets and showers, to make sure no one was there. This sort of scanning and checking was also performed in public places, such as parking garages. Some women had a whole method of walking quickly and having their keys ready. The men at the reading group said they never checked their homes or scanned garages. They never even considered such a thing.

- In Greta Gaard's *The Nature of Home: Taking Root in a Place*, she describes a job interview that included a tour of the city by a member of the hiring committee. During the tour, she is shown a nature area by a lake where she imagines jogging with her dog or taking evening walks. Then she wonders, "Were the lake's trails a safe shelter for women?"[5] She discovers the answer is no. Rapes have occurred there.

- When I was living alone, my boyfriend suggested I should go to the Goodwill and get a used pair of men's work boots to leave at my front door. This was kind and helpful advice. The men's boots may be a deterrent for someone wishing to break in or harm me.

- While on a solo road trip through Wyoming, one of my destinations that I was the most excited about visiting was the Medicine Wheel located in Bighorn National Forest. I planned this trip for months and it wasn't until a few days before I was leaving that I considered the area may be too remote. I read that I would need to park my car and walk a considerable distance to the site. I talked about this with my friend. If I reached the parking area and no one was there, we concluded it may not be safe enough for me to get out of my car. I would need to just leave. If I reached it and only saw a man or several men there, I would definitely not get out of my car. It would only be safe to make the journey from my car if other women were around. It turned out that snow prevented me from even reaching the Medicine Wheel, so I didn't get the opportunity to do this ridiculous, but required, surveillance.

- In 2017, I read women's rights activist Nicholas Kristof's brave article, "Husbands Are Deadlier than Terrorists,"[6] with such sadness, although I celebrated his courage and honesty, and then, with a much heavier sadness, I read the many hostile comments directed at him by gun

5 Greta Gaard, *The Nature of Home: Taking Root in a Place* (Tucson, AZ: University of Arizona Press, 2007), 11.

6 Nicholas Kristof, "Husbands are Deadlier than Terrorists," *New York Times*, Feb. 12, 2017, 11.

advocates and others on *The New York Times* website. Here was a man willing to publically state the obvious that is rarely stated. Here was a man willing to state why women are being killed. Here was a man who people directed hatred at for pointing out some facts that revealed horrible truths about violence against women in the United States.

Understanding Feminism

The examples above show us a few things. They demonstrate that when a woman is a victim of violence there is often a kneejerk reaction to want to place some or all of the blame on her. Perhaps she drank too much. Perhaps she was wearing revealing clothing. Perhaps she was out too late. These examples also show that a woman achieving something may be questioned. There is a possibility, this type of thinking suggests, that she may not have done so through her own grit and intellect. Perhaps she was helped out of pity. Perhaps she provided a sexual favor. Or maybe her success comes solely from how she looks.

Beyond these revelations, the examples also reveal that women often navigate their lives differently than men and this need to navigate is not only common, but it is restrictive. It limits even strong, independent women's abilities at times, but it is often just accepted and possibly not even thought about. Such is the life of a woman. Of course, the overarching reason for the time and energy surrounding these female navigations is fear of a violent attack by a man. The examples above also show us that there is a lot of violence against women in our world. I've heard arguments against feminism in the United States, because women can drive, live on their own, get educated, buy a home without a man, and work. Yes, these things are all true, but women also get raped and killed at alarming numbers.

It is easy to find misleading and detestable representations of feminism. For example, if someone is a woman and a feminist, she probably hates men. (Even though there are many awesome male feminists and allies.) She is probably nasty and unattractive. She may be a lesbian, which, in the views of such people, is also an abomination. And, ultimately, she is horribly misinformed. You see, it is often explained to such foolish women, often characterized as angry, that there is no need for feminism. Yes, anger may be a part of feminism, but shouldn't we all be angry about sexism, rape, and other forms of violence against women? Shouldn't we all be angry about inequality? We shouldn't dismiss someone's feminism because the individual displays emotion or anger. Wouldn't it be more appropriate to ask the one who is dismissing, "Why aren't you angry? Why aren't you upset about violence? Why aren't you upset about inequality?"

This leads to asking, if feminism isn't those characterizations mentioned before, what, really, is it? How do we define it? In *Feminism is for Everybody: Passionate Politics*, bell hooks writes, "Simply put, feminism is a movement to end sexism, sexist exploitation, and oppression."[7] If we think of feminism in this way, as a movement toward freedom, we understand feminism is positive and full of possibilities. It is the type of imagining of feminism Sara Ahmed writes about when she declares that hearing the word feminism fills her "with hope, with energy. It brings to mind loud acts of refusal and rebellion as well as the quiet ways we might have of not holding on to things that diminish us."[8] This is the understanding and embrace of feminism that is essential to Love Activism.

Male Violence

When we consider the examples of violence against women mentioned earlier or the ways women navigate their lives to prevent being attacked, it is often the case that the reason is not specifically stated. The culture of the United States, at least, has a difficult time simply addressing the problem. The problem is male violence. This does not mean, of course, that women cannot be violent. Of course a woman can be violent through physical actions or hateful speech and threats just like a man. And, a man can be a victim of violence. It is a known fact though that most horrific violent crime, including rapes, murders, and mass shootings, are committed by men. In the United States, 90 percent of all murders and 98 percent of all mass shootings are committed by men.[9] Since the majority of mass shootings are also committed by white men, this creates even more of a silencing around the country's horrific epidemic. (In 2017, the United States suffered

---

7 bell hooks, *Feminism is for Everybody: Passionate Politics* (Brooklyn, NY: South End Press, 2000), 1.

8 Sara Ahmed, *Living a Feminist Life* (Durham, NC: Duke University Press, 2017), 1.

9 John Haltiwanger, "White Men Have Committed More Mass Shootings than Any Other Group," *Newsweek.com*, Oct. 2, 2017, http://www.newsweek.com/white-men-have-committed-more-mass-shootings-any-other-group-675602

273 mass shootings where four or more people were killed or wounded.[10])
Why are there not more discussions about this?

Living in a violent culture impacts all of us, but it particularly restricts
women's lives. With male violence comes an inability for women to go
about their lives completely free. It is so ingrained and normalized, however, that even women often do not stop to think why they need to walk
quickly and with intent through a dark parking garage or why they feel a
sense of relief when they notice figures approaching on a dark street are
women. Women may also make decisions about their lives, such as where
to walk, how late to be out, where to travel, where to attend school, and so
on, for safety reasons that are almost always because of the unspoken fear
of rape and other forms of male violence. It would be helpful if all of us
openly discussed this issue. If we cannot speak the truth, all genders will
continue to suffer. Until we see an end to this male violence and the suffering and oppression it causes on a global scale, feminism is necessary.

The Importance of Intersectionality

Once while traveling I visited an art gallery to see an exhibit related to
working women. I believe this gallery does amazing work, but while
viewing this particular exhibit, it was clear that many women's stories were
not represented. The exhibit focused on the changing role of women in
the workforce with much discussion of the boom over the decades since
1950. Yes, it is true that significantly more women are in the labor force
now than in previous generations, but that is not the case in my family's
story and many others. My great grandmother, grandmother, and mother
all worked. According to the U.S. Bureau of Labor Statistics, 56.8% of
all women were working in 2016, whereas a much smaller percentage of
32.7% of all women worked in 1948.[11] Still, that 32.7% contains a lot of
stories, including my mom and grandma who would have been working
in 1948. Starting in 1972, when race and ethnicity were added to the sta-
tistical data, we can also see that 48.7% of black women were working

10 Naaz Modan, "How America Has Silently Accepted the Rage of
   White Men," *CNN.com*, Oct. 3, 2017, http://www.newsweek.com/
   white-men-have-committed-more-mass-shootings-any-other-group-675602

11 Statistics were pulled from the Women's Bureau of the United States Department of Labor,
   "Women in the Labor Force," charts available at https://www.dol.gov/wb/stats/NEWSTATS/
   facts/women_lf.htm

as opposed to 43.2% of white women. It frustrated me that the reality of so many women's experiences was not fairly represented. Another narrative often surrounding women's entry into the workforce is that it is something of a choice and power and that women were not able to exercise this freedom in previous generations due to oppressive forces. Some of that narrative is absolutely true, but definitely not all. It is important to consider that some women also had economic safety nets. Even if work was a possibility, it may not have been necessary to keep themselves and their family afloat. Many women from lower economic classes did not (and *do* not) have a choice. Their work is necessary for survival. One has to ultimately ask then, "Whose stories dominated the exhibit?"

Economic class, of course, is just one aspect of a person's identity. We need to always be aware of the different elements that construct each of our identities, which makes our activism and feminism inclusive and gets to the heart of what intersectionality means. Flavia Dzodan wrote a compelling and recommended piece titled, "My Feminism Will Be Intersectional or It Will Be Bullshit."[12] From South America, Dzodan describes herself as an "immigrant living in Europe." Her piece outlines the sadness and anger she experienced over a sample one week period after witnessing racist actions by white feminists. Then, when expressing outrage over racism, Dzodan found herself being told she was "divisive" and a "bad feminist." A feminist movement that requires women of color to forgive racism and focus only on gender will collapse by its unwillingness to embrace all elements, or intersections, of women's identities. Dzodan beautifully calls for an active engagement in "multi dimensional analysis."

Several decades before Dzodan found herself attacked for pointing out racism within feminism, Audre Lorde wrote of a similar experience. Lorde, a strong voice against a historically racist and ultimately exclusive white feminism, wrote, "Tomorrow belongs to those of us who conceive of it as belonging to everyone; who lend the best of ourselves to it, and with joy."[13] In one exclusionary example that clearly failed to embrace everyone in its feminist vision, Lorde writes of the First International Feminist Bookfair in London in 1984. Lorde was very excited about this momentous event, because she loved bookfairs and, being from the United States, she looked forward to meeting black feminists in London. It is her excitement that

12 Flavia Dzodan, "My Feminism Will Be Intersectional or It Will Be Bullshit," *Tiger Beatdown*, Oct. 10, 2011, http://tigerbeatdown.com/2011/10/10/my-feminism-will-be-intersectional-or-it-will-be-bullshit

13 Lorde, *A Burst of Light*, 99.

makes the story even more heartbreaking. At the event, Lorde found that the white women who organized it did not include any local black women. Her desire to discuss this, as in the past when similar racist and exclusionary things occurred, was seen as solely negative and destructive to the feminist cause instead of actually helping to build a better movement. Lorde wrote, "Feminism must be on the cutting edge of real social change if it is to survive as a movement in any particular country."[14] The issues that impact all women need to be represented. A thriving feminist movement must work to continuously explore and question what it can do better as an intersectional activism. Individual feminists must also conduct the same self-examination. Self-critique will not cause the demise of feminism. The opposite is true: an inability to critically and honestly examine will eventually cause a collapse when people see their experiences and opinions are not valued.

Ecofeminism

Since Love Activism is concerned with the earth and all living beings, ecofeminism is a form of feminism that is important to mention here. Ecofeminism is a holistic form that goes beyond human beings and seeks to understand and eradicate all forms of oppression brought about under a patriarchal structure. There are many ways to define ecofeminism. Since ecofemininsts see the destruction of the environment as the work of a dominant, male-centered paradigm, ecofeminism could be understood as environmentalism seen through the lens of feminism. Ecofeminism is also a feminism concerned with the relationship between human and non-human beings, often desiring the abolition of hierarchical constructs and dualities that result in the killing and annihilation of other species and the earth. Irene Diamond and Gloria Feman Orenstein write that "ecofeminism seeks to reweave new stories that acknowledge and value the biological and cultural diversity that sustains all life,"[15] as well as critique dualities such as human/animal and reason/emotion. It is for this reason that many ecofeminists, such as Carol J. Adams, are also vegan and animal rights activists. Ecofeminist Charlene Spretnak explains, "to care empathetically about the

---

14 Lorde, 64.

15 Irene Diamond and Gloria Feman Orenstein, "Introduction," in *Reweaving the World: The Emergence of Ecofeminism*, eds. Irene Diamond and Gloria Feman Orenstein (San Francisco, CA: Sierra Club Books, 1990), xi.

person, the species, and the great family of all beings, about the bioregion, the biosphere, and the universe is the framework within which ecofeminists wish to address the issues of our time."[16] Considering the large scale of this form of feminism, there are an abundance of issues and possibilities for activism. Ecofeminist Vandana Shiva's work is an excellent example.

Shiva's activism highlights how issues that negatively impact the natural world are intertwined with, and are causes of violence and oppression to human beings, and especially women. Working for a peaceful and sustainable world, Shiva has written several important works that highlight issues with food justice and women's rights, including *Earth Democracy: Justice, Sustainability and Peace*[17] and *Staying Alive: Women, Ecology, and Development*.[18] Advocating for "earth democracy," she focuses on seed, food, and water.[19] This includes activism against the privatization of water, industrialized agriculture, conversion of common land to enclosed private zones, production of genetically-modified crops, and seed patents. Although faced with such large structures and systems of opposition, Shiva speaks with resilience and hope: "Through everyday actions on everyday issues, we are creating living economies, living democracies, and living cultures." It is "through everyday actions," she tells us, that "we reweave the web of life."[20]

Practices of Feminism: reject sexist jokes; do not critique women's bodies; study women's history and feminism; support feminist presses and bookstores; read memoirs and autobiographies of women from diverse cultures and economic backgrounds; speak out against violence against women; donate clothing or other goods to a domestic violence shelter; create or join a feminist consciousness-raising group; read and research to become aware of global crimes against women...

---

16 Charlene Spretnak, "Ecofeminism: Our Roots and Flowering," in *Reweaving the World: The Emergence of Ecofeminism*, eds. Irene Diamond and Gloria Feman Orenstein (San Francisco, CA: Sierra Club Books, 1990), 12.

17 Vandana Shiva, *Earth Democracy: Justice, Sustainability, and Peace* (Berkeley, CA: North Atlantic Books, 2005).

18 Vandana, Shiva, *Staying Alive: Women, Ecology, and Development* (Berkeley, CA: North Atlantic Books, 2016).

19 Shiva, *Earth Democracy*, 129.

20 Shiva, 129.

Mindfulness

Colors: cream, white, gold

Mindfulness is when we are able to remain in the present moment and free our minds of anxiety, fear, depression, and other harmful emotions that are often the result of worrying about the past or future. Mare Chapman, a practitioner and educator of mindfulness, explains that mindfulness is "about waking up from the trance of our conditioning, so we can know ourselves more deeply and wisely."[1] Being mindful can make our activism more attentive, focused, and aware. Mindfulness may not come easy to us, but may be cultivated through meditation, yoga, or many other practices offered as ideas below.

Eating

For the four decades I was able to share with my mom, one thing she never failed to do was to close her eyes and say a silent prayer before any meal or snack in private or public settings. I even saw her do this before drinking a cup of tea or glass of water. This peaceful gesture was a way of grounding herself and demonstrating gratitude. She would have never used the word "mindfulness," but clearly her practice falls under this umbrella.

In Starhawk's *The Earth Path,* she provides instructions for a practice called "Cooking and Eating with Gratitude," which reminds me of my mom's silent prayer. Starhawk's practice involves stopping, giving thanks, and blessing the food before starting to eat. She writes, "Ground and

---

1 Chapman, *Unshakeable Confidence,* 70.

come into your senses before you eat. Eat consciously, savoring the taste and noticing the energy of what you take in."[2] A form of gratitude and blessing may also be given for the farmworkers or any individuals whose work brought the food to your table.

At a former workplace, most of us were overworked and underpaid and the days could go by stressfully and quickly. A co-worker and friend who was trying to keep up like the rest of us had a daily ritual that I encountered by surprise one day. I went to her office while she was eating lunch and found she had cleared a space amongst the piles of paperwork and files to place a cloth table setting. There she had an actual glass (not a plastic throw-away cup or bottle), silverware, a cloth napkin, and a ceramic salad bowl. This ritual, which truly only took a few extra minutes to arrange each day, made lunch a beautiful and calming ceremony. It also brought focus to what was happening.

Another possibility for mindful action while eating is enjoying a silent meal. I first experienced the wonder of a silent meal while at a women's yoga and writing retreat. Although we were silent at this retreat while writing and meditating, once we were eating or going about the rest of our days, conversation was in abundance. Of course, much of this was joyful and helpful conversation. The leaders of the retreat decided we would gather for a silent dinner one night. How profoundly different it was to sit with all of these women and simply eat in silence. We discussed our experience after. Although some women felt uncomfortable at first, there was no denying that for many of us the silence offered an unexpected and deep connection with each other and our food.

What else can we do in regards to mindfulness and eating? In *How to Eat,* Thich Nhat Hanh brings the whole universe into his mindfulness practice by considering how the earth and the sky are part of each spoonful. When eating an apple, he considers the seed, the orchard, the farmworker, the sky, and so on.[3] While drinking a cup of tea, he meditates on how he is also drinking the rain and the clouds. "The way we drink our tea can transform our lives if we truly devote our attention to it,"[4] he writes. He also offers that mindfulness practice can extend beyond just eating, to the preparation of the food and the cleaning up, including even washing the dishes.

---

2 Starhawk, *The Earth Path*, 119.

3 Hanh, *How to Eat*, 8-9.

4 Hanh, 84.

I chose to start this mindfulness chapter with eating because, even if we do not feel we have time to cultivate mindfulness in our lives, there is a guarantee that we will all take time to eat each day and this offers us a chance to make new rituals and ground ourselves in the present moment a few times daily. You may do an experiment the next several times you eat while following your regular routine. Is there a lot of commotion around you? Is the radio or television on? Are there other types of distracting sounds competing for your mental focus? Do you look at your phone, your computer, or a book while eating by yourself or even with others? Are you often doing another activity while eating? Consider how you may be able to introduce a mindfulness practice at these moments for yourself and possibly for your partner and family. Another possibility is to gather with friends or your partner and share a silent meal. You may be surprised, as I was, with how deeply connected you feel with your food and those around you. The silence provides another layer of nourishment beyond the food.

Celebrating Everyday Magic

As we enrich our mindfulness practice, we become more aware and able to see the everyday magic and beauty of simple things. It is as if a new way of seeing opens up. Being less distracted, we can take in what is right in front of us. Not only do we see people more clearly, but common things such as a cup of coffee or an orange take on a new richness and depth. Seeing the magic in everyday objects and the rituals that go along with our days helps to live more simple lives that exist in opposition to the throwaway consumer culture that always desires something more and something new.

One of the best illustrations of celebrating everyday magic is found in the poetry of Pablo Neruda. In his *Elemental Odes* or *Odes to Common Things*,[5] Neruda's poems celebrate objects that we may think of us mundane and inconsequential, but he demonstrates how they actually carry much depth. In "Ode to the Bed,"[6] he imagines the bed as a companion on our life journey; in "Ode to the Table,"[7] he sees an entire world; and

---

5 Pablo Neruda, *Odes to Common Things* (New York, NY: Bulfinch Press, 2013).

6 Neruda, 29-31.

7 Neruda, 19-21.

"Ode to the Tomato"[8] takes us through streets until a magical salad is created. Neruda's *Odes to Common Things* also include poems written for the onion, the artichoke, bread, a pair of scissors, and much more. In the beginning of his "Ode to Things," the poet confesses, "I have a crazy, / crazy love of things."[9] Neruda, often thought of for his love sonnets and political poems, was obviously a connoisseur of everyday magic. Reading his poetry, which is accessible to most of us through his use of everyday language, can bring a new awareness and focus to our lives.

Thomas Moore's *The Re-enchantment of Everyday Life* is another example of everyday magic. In this book, Moore shares that "an enchanted life has many moments when the heart is overwhelmed by beauty and the imagination is electrified..."[10] He suggests that, to restore enchantment, we need "to recover a beginner's mind and a child's wonder."[11] Food, bookstores, stones, water, trees, and more objects, things in the natural world, and places are suggested by Moore as avenues of re-enchantment. As activists, when faced with setbacks and difficulties, bringing mindfulness and magic to our everyday lives can help build sustenance.

Cultivating Silence or Quiet

An important part of mindfulness practice is to cultivate silence or quiet in our lives. This was touched on briefly in the discussion above on eating, but can be brought into other areas of our lives. This is an ongoing commitment for many of us, due to where we live. It is hard to find quiet places in urban areas and considerably more challenging to find ones we could call silent. Having lived in Southern California since elementary school, the freeway, for example, is a constant sound. Even when I lived over a mile away from a freeway I could still often hear it. And then there are other noises all around us. In some areas of Los Angeles, when walking down the sidewalk, loud dance or pop music comes at you from different stores. Over time, we may hardly even notice some of these obtrusive sounds; they simply become part of our daily realities. Because of them, we may even find ourselves continuing the noise in our homes. We become accustomed to distraction.

---

8 Neruda, 141-145.

9 Neruda, 11.

10 Thomas Moore, *The Re-enchantment of Everyday Life* (New York, NY: HarperPerennial, 1996), ix.

11 Moore, xx.

Over the last several years I have noticed some additional noises being added to our already chaotic environments. The first development was when I was waiting in line at a grocery store and I heard televisions. There in the check-out lines were televisions playing commercials. I then discovered these televisions at gas stations while pumping gas. Another discovery was when I parked my car at a large shopping center. I heard music. Yes, even in the parking lot, music was being played through speakers. At another shopping and restaurant location, I suppose to make visitors feel that they are out in the wilderness, I heard frog and cricket sounds around the grounds. It is as if we can never be alone with our thoughts. Distractions are everywhere. If we live in the country, we may have more peace and quiet when we are outside, but we may have noisy environments in our homes with televisions constantly running, even when guests are over.

It is interesting to see what happens when we remove ourselves from noise and go to a place that is completely silent. I've experienced different things that were unexpected when I've done this. My first experience was when I traveled to Kentucky to stay one week at the monastery where Thomas Merton used to live. At the time, I was around thirty-two years old and I had been practicing a form of Catholic meditation called centering prayer. I was very devoted to my practice, meditating twice each day, before and after work, for periods of twenty minutes. From doing this, I noticed I handled stress better and was able to calm my emotions well when faced with a nuisance or difficulty. I thought I was quite the master at this meditation and silence stuff. What I didn't really notice was that there were still many noises around when I was meditating, such as people walking by on the sidewalk near my apartment, cars buzzing by on a busy street, and, the nosiest element: the city bus stop just a few feet from where I lived.

The monastery in Kentucky was silent except for a few places, such as the office and lobby area where guests arrived. There was also no cell service on the monastery grounds or the surrounding area at the time of my trip. The rooms, of course, had no radios or televisions and since I was by myself I was completely in silence in my room. I brought a suitcase full of books with plans to read and go for walks while immersing myself in the monastery life. What happened almost immediately was that I was tired and found the need to take several naps during the day. I don't remember reading much. I mostly walked around the grounds throughout the day and went to my room for naps. I believe it was on the third day that the silence really got to me. I left the monastery in the pick-up truck I rented and drove about 130 miles to Cincinnati, Ohio. I walked around a little, hearing all the sounds of the city, and then I got in the truck and drove back to the monastery. After this experience I spoke to a monk in the office and lobby area about the silence and how I was so tired even though I was doing nothing. He told me he commonly hears what I described, because we do not realize how tired our bodies are and how busy and full of distractions and noise our lives are until we are completely removed from everything. I ended up wishing I had longer to stay. Once I returned to my life in California, I missed the peacefulness of the monastery and longed for it, even though I could not fully enjoy it for much of the time I was there.

A similar thing happened about four years ago when I went to a silent monastery near Big Sur, California. Once again, I was in a room with no radio or television and when I encountered people on the grounds we would remain silent. On day two I found myself stir crazy. I left the monastery to go to Carmel, about an hour away. Once I got to Carmel and experienced an issue with parking and some other nuisances, I felt I was wasting my time and acting foolishly when I could have been at the peaceful monastery. I remember going into a restaurant and everything seemed so noisy. I drove back to the monastery after a short time. Like all those years before, when I returned, I went to a designated area where I could speak and I told a monk about my restlessness and my ridiculous adventure to Carmel. He said, "At least you didn't drive the whole way to Los Angeles." "No," I said, "That's where I came from." We laughed about this.

These experiences, although not what I planned, told me a lot about myself and my regular environment. When you consider your different environments, do you find it is typically noisy, quiet, or silent? Are you able to experiment with silence, or, at least, quiet, but turning off radios, televisions, or other common distractions? Is there some other type of adjustment you may be able to make to reduce the level of noise around you?

Thomas Moore connects silence with listening. He writes, "Silent listening is a particular way of being active, not passive, in the world." He continues, "In silence we can hear subtle sounds that are usually drowned out by the cacophony generated by a technology culture."[12] Silence, understood and experienced in this way, is not really an absence of sound. In fact, it heightens our awareness and brings our attention to things we may not otherwise notice. This connection of silence and listening moves right into the concept of deep listening.

---

12 Moore, 104.

Deep Listening

Not long ago I was eating at a restaurant in Venice Beach, California, and the person I was with said, "Look around. Everyone is on their phones." It was true. I looked around the crowded interior to discover people were looking at their phones at almost every table. Some people were talking to each other while looking at their phones and others were not talking, but engrossed with their phones. Obviously, there are times when we may need to look at our phones for something, but I was struck with how many people did not seem to be fully present with the people around them. The restaurant was also very beautiful, so I wondered if they were also not taking the time to enjoy the beauty around them. Were the people in conversation able to deeply listen to each other while multitasking? In the chapter on service I discussed deep listening within the context of presence and how easy it is to be distracted. How can we improve this?

Practices such as meditation can clearly help, as well as doing what we can to remove distractions, but specific deep listening exercises can also be very beneficial here. The composer Pauline Oliveros' lifelong practice was deep listening. In her book, *Deep Listening: A Composer's Sound Practice*, Oliveros outlines a beautiful and quite extensive practice. She points out the difference between hearing and listening, stating, "To hear is the physical means that enables perception. To listen is to give attention to what is perceived both acoustically and psychologically."[13] She also believes that both "compassion (spiritual development) and understanding comes from listening impartially to the whole space/time continuum of sound..."[14] Within the wealth of exercises she provides, some are lists of profound questions. Here are a few examples: "Are you listening while you are hearing?;" "What causes you to listen?;" "What is the soundscape of your neighborhood?;" and "Are you sure that you are hearing everything that there is to hear?"[15] It is clear to see how these questions on listening can impact our awareness and activism.

---

13 Pauline Oliveros, *Deep Listening: A Composer's Sound Practice* (New York, NY: iUniverse, 2005), xxii.

14 Oliveros, xxv.

15 Oilveros, 34, 56.

Practices of Mindfulness: be deeply present for someone; eat some silent meals; turn off the television/get rid of your television; meditate; say a gratitude statement or prayer before eating; offer kind and authentic self-expression; offer/practice deep listening; have moments of silence in your life; refrain from major decisions when you are confused...

Living Portraits: Interviews With Activists

On the following pages we will discover some incredible individuals who are inspiring activists in their communities. How exciting to consider that these beautiful souls are alive right now and actively working toward a more peaceful and just world. The ten activists included illustrate different ways of performing activism and are presented to provide inspiration and stimulate new ideas. Their work provides practical and creative applications of different elements of Love Activism.

Elise Bernal

Artist and Art Educator
Pico Rivera, California

"I've learned that you can use whatever knowledge you have to help people be empowered."

Can you tell me about your work as an artist and art educator?

As an artist, I make zines, little clay sculptures, and textile creatures and wall hangings. My work is about sharing things that I've learned by listening to myself or others. Recently my practice has shifted to focus on building community in whatever way I can. I am realizing that certain spaces have the potential to bring out amazing parts of people. Right now, I'm trying to figure out how to create more spaces like that, so that people feel safe and can share the best parts of themselves. A lot of the time, I think we are all just in need of a space where we can reach those parts.

What type of art education have you done with children?

I have worked at a few museums where I have led family programming, children's workshops, and tours focused on art-making and writing. I also recently started working for an arts council where programming focuses on learning about and creating public art with third graders. I also host freelance classes and workshops that are focused on DIY methods. For me, art education is really about sustainable practices, meaning things that you can talk about or do yourself that are awesome and connect you to new ideas, but are also practices you can keep doing to be empowered.

A good experience I had was teaching DIY screen-printing at the LGBTQ Center in Long Beach. I went back to visit and all the kids are still screen-printing. They're making their own T-shirts and posters. It's cool to see it being accessible and that they're able to be creative and use their voice. I've learned that you can use whatever knowledge you have to help people be empowered.

Much of your work seems to be about self-care. Can you tell me about this?

My focus on self-care is something I learned more about within the past couple of years. I think a big part of that was seeing my mom go through cancer treatment. It inspired me to be more patient and really listen, and that got me connected more with mindfulness practices. When I think of self-care, it is things that you can take with you and use when you need them. The word that's been in my mind more recently is "tools." Tools don't look the same for everyone. I think of my tiny zines as tools people can use to take a moment to smile and feel empowered.

Can you tell me about the Self-Care Share opening?

I was invited to do a residency for the Institute for Labor Generosity Workers and Uniforms (ILGWU). One of their projects, Sewing Rebellion, is a bimonthly workshop to empower people to learn to sew. The focus of the opening was a large wall hanging in the form of a body. Each of the pockets was in the form of a different body part, and each thing inside that pocket was something that was learned through an interaction with that body part. Anyone visiting could take what they wanted from the pockets. For example, I had a funny bone that was filled with really cheesy jokes and a pocket that resembled a boob (some people thought it was a lung and I was cool with that, too), that held a zine that I compiled with resources for cancer patients and families. In the head were little notes about remembering that you're an important part of the world; I saw them as little thoughts. I wanted people to interact with it and have their own experience, literally taking away what they felt was important. The body itself became a community body, a community space for conversations on self-care and healing.

Can you tell me about the community cook and conversations that you created?

My original intention was to ask people not to bring any money, but bring an ingredient to contribute, and then, with the ingredients everyone brought, we would make a meal together and learn how to cook some-thing. The thing that we would cook would be based on a food that was important to whoever was hosting it, whether that was culturally important or just a personal emotional connection to the food. The first one I had was at my house in Pico Rivera. We made tamales. I actually had never made them before, but it was a really important food to me, because my grandma would always make them. We made a vegetarian version, so everyone could enjoy it. People were grinding the masa. People were manning the pot. Together we would each do little steps to make it happen. Each of us was able to make our own tamale by spreading the masa and stuffing it with whatever we wanted. After that we sat down and we talked about what the experience was like cooking together.

I also had a little station for when people arrived. They could write a question that they would like to ask someone. Everyone chose a question someone had asked, and then we went in a circle and everybody answered their question. It ranged from really personal things to memories with food or even something like, "What's your favorite color?" It was a combination of getting people together to enjoy food in a different way and also learn about the history of the food and create memories together. In the political space where we are now, it's hard to recognize that we do need to have these moments of joy and self-care to keep us motivated and keep us moving. It's important to know that when we come together we're empowered in these different ways.

Tell me about someone you admire.

I admire so many people, because I feel like we are meant to know every person who comes into our lives for a reason. One of those people is my grandma, Ruth. She's gone through a lot in her life, but even at age 84 she's still so feisty. She has this way of communicating to people where they feel like, "All right. We're not different. We're just here together and we're both people." I really admire that characteristic in her. It's something I'm still learning.

Discover more about Elise's art at www.etsy.com/shop/elisebee

Allister Chang

Executive Director, Libraries Without Borders
Washington, D. C.

"I think people are most vulnerable when they don't have full access to information."

What is the mission of Libraries Without Borders?

Libraries Without Boarders is a non-profit whose mission is to expand access to information and education for disadvantaged communities. We have worked in over 35 countries. Our work has focused on isolated and low-income communities, as well as communities that have recently suffered from natural or political disaster. For example, we worked in Haiti after the earthquake and currently work in Colombia as part of the peace-building process. In the United States we are doing work in the lowest-income congressional districts, including The Bronx and southwest Detroit. Those programs look different than those that we run in the African Great Lakes or West Africa, but the mission is very similar, which is to equip local communities with knowledge-based tools that increase opportunities.

Please tell me about the Ideas Box.

The Ideas Box is a pop-up media center and digital classroom that sits on two standard transportation pallets when it's closed. It's easy to ship with standard costs. When it opens, the shell of the box, which is waterproof, becomes the furniture for a space that fits up to 80 people. This is a fully-comprehensive small library and media center with its own power source;

satellite connection; and furniture, which includes tables and chairs. There is also multi-media curated content, ranging from paper books to tablets and video cameras and a TV screen. All the technology is connected via the server that we make in-house. It's loaded with curated software.

Where are some locations where you have brought the Ideas Box?

We have implemented Ideas Box programs in contexts as varied as refugee camps in Burundi to the mountains and jungles of Colombia. In France, we have created Ideas Box programs in homeless shelters. In the U.S., we've had the Ideas Box in public parks and laundromats. It is a very versatile tool. The bulk of the work is in building relationships with local organizations, so that they can make the tool kit their own as a way to expand their capacity to reach more audiences and new audiences with greater impact.

How have you been able to determine the success of the Ideas Box?

The project in Burundi is the longest standing and provides the most evidence. We've evaluated the impact with a few different tests that look at the education scores for K-12 students, as well as a more qualitative psychosocial review of how access to the tools and space provided by the Ideas Box supports the psychosocial health of refugees in Burundi. We have seen positive results. In Detroit, we also did an education test-based evaluation with positive results. Education and test scores are one of the easier ways to evaluate impact, although it is only one of several ways in which we see the Ideas Box adding value for our local community partners.

Please tell me about another project that the organization has been involved with.

In the U.S., we are partnering with the Coin Laundry Association, which is a trade group of laundromat owners around the U.S. We want to turn laundromats into lifelong learning spaces where the laundromat owners work with us to create pop-up libraries and media center spaces within laundromats. The libraries and media centers will have curated content that is timed for users to be able to complete sessions between wash and dry cycles. Our goal with this one is to be able to work with families who might not have time to go to the library. Maybe they have transportation barriers to get to the library and access library programs. With this project, they will be able to access content when they are idle and waiting for their laundry to wash and dry.

Do libraries partner with you on any of your projects?

Yes. That is very important for us, because we want to make sure that we are complementing what libraries are already doing, as well as thinking about long-term sustainability for our programs. We want to connect with broader strategies of the local library system and the city.

How did you get involved in this kind of work?

My background is in public policy and human rights. What I found doing human rights work is that the root cause of problems often comes back to this question of access to reliable information. I think people are most vulnerable when they don't have full access to information. This issue kept coming up in my work. I have been very interested in focusing on that particular aspect of how we protect vulnerable populations.

Who is someone you admire?

A very inspirational person for me is Kyle Zimmer. She is the founder of First Book, which is an incredible organization that is also based in D.C. First Book has created an innovative social enterprise model to make reading materials more accessible.

Discover more about Libraries Without Borders at
www.librarieswithoutborders.org

Dawn Finley

Co-founder, Feminist Library on Wheels (F.L.O.W.)
Los Angeles, California

"F.L.O.W. has been an amazing vehicle for me to be able to participate in creating change and helping other people."

Please tell me about F.L.O.W.

F.L.O.W., the Feminist Library on Wheels, is a mobile lending library with a collection of almost 5,000 donated items, including books, movies, zines, and ephemera. The materials can be checked out by anyone who signs up for a library card. It's completely free. People can check out as many items as they want and keep them for as long as they want. It's all on the honor system. Our main branch is at the Women's Center for Creative Work in Frogtown, Los Angeles, but we have drop-off locations all over the city for people to return items or bring donations. Some of our drop-off locations are independent bookstores, so people can even support a local business by buying a donation for F.L.O.W. We also try to get out as much as we can at different events around town to make the collection more accessible. Right now we're trying to find more organizations who might like to have a small branch to help us really expand the availability of the library to more people around the city.

How did F.L.O.W. get started?

In July of 2014, Jenn Witte and I were in the feminist reading group that I help to facilitate for the Women's Center for Creative Work. Jenn, who works at Skylight Books in Los Feliz, was talking to the WCCW about building a library for them. She brought that idea to the reading group and added that maybe the library could be on her bike. When she said that, I raised my hand and said, "Whatever you want, I'll help you!" I had just gotten into cycling at the time and was looking for a way to do cycling advocacy. The idea of doing feminist advocacy in addition seemed too good to be true. Many dots became connected to each other very, very quickly.

We did not, in our wildest dreams, expect to grow as much and as quickly as we did. We get donations almost daily. It has really amazed us. We don't tell people what feminism is. We give people a tool they can use to figure that out for themselves. Because the books are all donated, we have a crowd-sourced definition of feminism. It's not what Jenn and I think feminism is; it's what all the people who donate to us think a feminist library should be.

Does the library actually go out sometimes on a bicycle?

Yes. We have a custom tricycle that was built very soon after F.L.O.W. started. It's an industrial trike that has a closed bookcase mounted on the back. We can fill it with books or we can bring the books separately and fill it later. What we'd really love is to be able to have the resources to get an electric assist cargo bike. Something like that would help us carry the books up L.A.'s hills, but also make riding for F.L.O.W. more accessible for different kinds of riders.

What are some of the subject areas in the library's collection?

We have a lot of biographies and autobiographies that represent quite a variety of women, amplifying the stories of women who have been neglected in other histories or other narratives about our culture. Beyond that, we really have a bit of everything, including religion, politics, history, humor, health, relationships, cooking, science, fiction, sports, and also books on the history of feminist movements, feminist theory, and feminist organizing.

How many people use the library?

We have close to 900 cardholders. We currently have around 850 books checked out.

Is there anything else you would like to share about your work with F.L.O.W.?

I'd love to be able to change the world by reading books on my own, but I know that's not going to happen. F.L.O.W. has been an amazing vehicle for me to be able to participate in creating change and helping other people. We've had a lot of people come up to us and say something like, "I really feel I should know more about feminism, but I don't know where to start." For us to be able to be there for people in that moment and give them an access point or a starting place is a very powerful thing. Through F.L.O.W., I experience a very definite feeling of being able to connect with people and being able to do something meaningful for them. I can't say enough about how grateful I am for that opportunity.

Can you tell me about someone who you admire?

One person I really admire is Teka-Lark Lo, now an organizer at New York-based cycling advocacy organization Transportation Alternatives. I met her through the Blk Grrl Book Fair, which she ran in 2015 and 2016. F.L.O.W. attended both years. I think it's only recently that I've started to understand how much I've learned from her. She has a real lucidity in her way of thinking about the world that I admire. She writes about race, feminism, anti-capitalism, and building healthy communities. She's a brave, astute thinker. In her organizing she centers the experiences and voices of people of color, people who are ignored by the business-as-usual of capitalism. What she does is fantastic.

Discover more about F.L.O.W. at feministlibraryonwheels.com and browse the library's collection at www.librarycat.org/lib/F.L.O.W.

Renee Folzenlogen

Art Therapist and Family Support Counselor
Montclair, New Jersey

"I believe that creativity is the birthright of every person."

When did you decide to become an art therapist and what led you to this type of work?

I've always loved art. I grew up in a family where the arts were very much appreciated. My mom gave me a book, *Art as Therapy with Children*, when I was 12, and it planted a seed for me.

Later in life, when my infant son was diagnosed with cancer, I found myself returning to my art practice as a way to get through the emotions that it brought up, including the grief and trauma from a mom's point of view. I called upon my creativity and used art for my own process of healing. That is when I fully entered my art therapy studies.

It is inspiring when people return to school to fulfill a dream. How old were you when you became licensed as an art therapist?

I was 54 when I became licensed. It took me a long time, about thirteen years, to complete my formal studies. I had to finish my bachelor's degree first and then I went on for my master's degree. One of the only reasons I was able to go back to school was because of the other moms who supported me. I had three children who were still toddlers and babies. We traded childcare and together we made it happen. I always think about other women who helped me to get my education.

Please tell me about some populations you have worked with as an art therapist.

Through my graduate internships, I provided art therapy for children experiencing bereavement, and with women and children affected by domestic violence. Currently I'm working with family members of adults who are living with persistent mental illness.

Art is an agent of healing. It immediately brings a transforming energy to whatever suffering or difficulty an individual is experiencing. As soon as you put a mark on the paper you are activating some kind of change, some sort of positive change towards that experience.

I believe that creativity is the birthright of every person. As adults, people may experience negative thoughts and not believe they can create and be artists. One of my roles is to help remove those roadblocks, and make art something that is safe and accessible. Everyone can access that power, which is our wisdom and ability to heal ourselves. Art therapy is one of the modalities that helps create the conditions for a person to experience this.

The challenges I have experienced in my own life give me greater understanding, and hopefully, greater compassion, that I can then bring to the next person whom I encounter. Through our difficulties, we discover the universal experience that is part of the human condition. We can help each other along.

What are some of the art therapy practices you bring to people?

Art therapy teaches you to trust the process. When you're doing any kind of activity you learn to find a comfort level with uncertainty and a tolerance for not quite knowing what's going to happen next. I use drawing materials, paint, clay, and found materials. I also use sandtray therapy, which is rooted in Jungian concepts where an individual intuitively works with figures and items in the sand.

Lately I've been using an altered book activity. You take a book that's already been published. Then, using your own hand, and the materials that you select, you add, embellish, and transform the printed pages, as if they were your canvas. The entire process can be dynamic and exciting, and it serves as a metaphor for writing your own story in life.

Whatever the medium I use, I try to give clients the tools to look at what they've created and dialogue with it. Whether it's a drawing, a painting, or a little scene that they've created in the sand, I'll guide a client with questions. What do you see? How does it make you feel? What are the thoughts that it brings up? The tradition of art therapy has taught me to say to people, "Never be afraid of the images that come up, because they're your allies." Carl Jung believed that these images are messengers of one's own inner wisdom. I love it when a person is surprised by what emerges. It may help them gain an insight or help them to be more compassionate with themselves and others. You really see movement happening.

Please tell me about someone you admire.

That's really easy for me. I admire my dad. He was an immigrant from Shanghai, China. Although my dad was raised under Confucianism, he took me to Catholic Mass every week, because he wanted me to be around people who were trying to live up to an ethical standard and follow their conscience. I learned so much from him about inclusion, compassion, respect, and diversity. He was alert up until just a few hours before he died at the age of 92. He lived with us and died here at home. My dad was so appreciative of the little things in life. He's a role model of strength to me through his kindness, compassion, and how he was open to and interested in people who were different from him.

Discover more about Renee at reneetamara.wordpress.com

Joel Garcia

Director of Programs and Operations
Self Help Graphics
Los Angeles, California

"Printmaking continues to be one of the more democratic mediums."

Self Help Graphics has been a part of the community for several decades. Can you tell me about its history?

Self Help Graphics came together through the work of Sister Karen Boccalero, Carlos Bueno, Frank Hernandez, and others as a way to provide artists with a space and resources to use art as a means of activism. Printmaking continues to be the foundation of everything that we do here. It has been an instrumental part of many movements, including the United Farm Workers. It's a medium that can be used to hijack the media and work against government propaganda and other oppressive bodies. Printmaking continues to be one of the more democratic mediums. It's easy to teach and it's inexpensive. Our projects have elevated the voices of many, including day laborers, queer men, those negatively impacted by gentrification, and indigenous peoples.

How did you get involved in this work?

I grew up a few blocks down the street at the Maravilla Projects. It's a housing project on the same street, Cesar Chavez, where the most well known site of Self Help Graphics was located. I would pass by there often and I knew it as an art space. As a teenager, I started going to punk shows there.

If you were an East LA artist, Self Help was where you would go and take workshops. It was also a space used for punk shows. It was through punk rock and events happening there that I was introduced to what Self Help was about. I started getting involved volunteering for the annual Day of the Dead celebrations, which are an important part of the community. I became politicized through punk rock and awakened culturally through the Day of the Dead. With my friends, I started organizing punk shows. That's how I got involved with Self Help.

Please tell me about a recent project of Self Help Graphics.

The project we did with day laborers stands out. We wanted to provide our resources to elevate their voices and highlight some of the struggles they face beyond what we see or might imagine. Through our printmaking program, which has been around for 35 years, we bring an artist in as part of a two-week residency to create a serigraph edition. They keep half of it so they can sell it and sustain themselves. The other half we keep to archive. We wanted to find day laborers who are artists, but are doing a type of work just to send money back home and sustain themselves here.

One thing we didn't anticipate was that we would find artists not just in LA, but around the nation. We thought it would take about one year to complete the project, including recruiting the artists and producing the serigraphs. It took us about a year and a half just to find 10 artists that would be willing and that could devote time to producing the serigraph.

Because this would become such a high profile project, some artists didn't want to risk being outed with an undocumented status. In other instances we found folks who were willing to participate, but didn't speak English or Spanish. We had funding from the NEA to bring folks to LA, but some artists didn't want to travel, because they didn't want to risk being deported if they were asked for documentation. We figured out ways to make it happen with translations and things like Skype and FaceTime to communicate.

Every individual created their piece that spoke to different issues. Examples include the process of getting to the U.S. and the experiences of stress, depression, and culture clash. One artist had a sole image of a hand. It was meant to call attention to all of the injuries that take place. Since they do not have Worker's Compensation benefits, there is no medical aide. They basically need to suck it up and go to work injured the next day or no money will be coming in. The project was impactful for me, because it was layered in so many different ways.

Can you tell me about the Barrio Mobile Art Studio?

The Barrio Mobile Art Studio was a program that was launched in the late 70s by Sister Karen with support from artist Linda Vallejo. Self Help has always been insistent on making art as accessible as possible to the community. This meant being able to go out to a park, school, or back alley to expose youth and the community to free art programs. The teaching methodology of the program has always been peer to peer instruction. This makes it more of a conversation between the artist and the community members. The artist acts as a guide through the process of creating something. The process is important, but it is also important that the participants see themselves as artists who are able to produce something. Because of budget cuts when Reagan came along, the program ceased to exist in the early to mid-80s. We relaunched it in 2014. Although we exist here in a physical space, it continues to be difficult for the entire community to come and participate in programming for different reasons. For youngsters, it might be because they're scared of crossing gang territories. Even though the metro is available for youth, it can be intimidating to be on a platform where you have sheriffs. There are different barriers.

We bought a 24-foot trailer that we keep pretty bare, so it is flexible and we can stock it with whatever art supplies are needed for mural painting, printmaking, or other projects. It's a cargo trailer that we pull with a truck. We've used it for workshops for smaller groups of 10 to 15 students up to as many as 400 students. It allows us to do a program for a whole school.

Since relaunching the program, we trained 25 artists to be able teach in that peer to peer pedagogy. We are now training a group of youth, ages 16 to about 24, to be able to facilitate workshops for their peers.

Who is someone you admire?

That would be Brett Gurewitz of Epitaph Records. Before Self Help, I worked there designing record covers. He instilled in his own artists the idea of artist development and artist nurturing. He taught me the business side of being an artist, including how to handle budgets and marketing. I saw what was possible, because of my time at Epitaph. I discovered that if you put the right tools around an artist they are going to be successful.

We all fall down at some point or another. It's how you get up and how you treat others when you're at your lowest point that matters the most. Brett has made mistakes, but he found ways to right those wrongs. He has a strong work ethic and I admire his approach to cultivating and nurturing creative minds. It informs the work I do here on a daily basis.

Discover more about Self Help Graphics at selfhelpgraphics.com

Nicole Landers

Director and Founding Member, Community Healing Gardens
Los Angeles, California

"Anyone in the community can touch, feel, smell, partake, and eat from the boxes we planted."

How did you get started with Community Healing Gardens and what is the mission of the organization?

Community Healing Gardens is a non-profit that launched in the summer of 2015 in Venice, California. The mission of the organization is to foster community and educate people on the importance of growing food through urban gardening. We believe every empty patch of soil has the potential to feed and educate about nutrition, sustainability, connection, healing, community, and love. We have a specific focus on diverse and underserved communities. We started by planting every other weekend from late June into September. We had people helping from all walks of life and all ages. There were women in their 80s and children as young as two-year-olds. Anyone in the community can touch, feel, smell, partake, and eat from the boxes we planted. We also have a goal to create organic urban gardens in schools throughout the Los Angeles Unified School District (LAUSD), especially in food desert neighborhoods. Ultimately, Community Healing Gardens provides healthy food, local jobs, education, and a positive solution to climate change while fostering community through a local volunteer movement.

My passion is health, well-being, and sustainability, especially the importance of nurturing nature within our communities. I've been living in Los Angeles for eighteen years and in Venice Beach for eight years now. I met a community member named Grant Gottfurcht who had this wild idea about how we could create unity in our community around growing food. We didn't ask for permission to plant street side. We just did it. That's how it started.

What types of fruits and vegetables do you grow?

A great thing that has come out of this is that we have some incredible urban farmers involved with the organization. It's a gift having people that do this for a living volunteering their time to help. We grow seasonally. We have grown strawberries, blueberries, kale, cucumbers, tomatoes, squash, and other fruits and vegetables. We also grow herbs, including chives, oregano, basil, lemon basil, thyme, rosemary, fennel, and more.

Besides people in the neighborhood eating from the boxes, where are some other places the food has gone?

There is a local community center that has a food bank. We have donated fresh produce to them. There are also some organizations we partner with; one is Safe Place for Youth. We help young adults to get off the street by providing job training. They can go off and work for a landscaper or start their own business. They can also grow food and work at farmer's markets. We're also working with the Saint Joseph Center, which is another organization in Venice that helps the homeless and challenged men and women. They have a 16-week culinary program that trains up to 20 men and women in a restaurant setting. They are going to use our food in this program, and also a few of the students will be interning with us.

Please tell me about your work with the middle school in Watts.

One of our volunteers has a summer camp in Watts at Edwin Markham Middle School. He invited us to visit the school and we did. It is mostly asphalt, but there is a piece of property on the backside of the school that had once been an orchard and working agriculture program. It is an acre of property that was lying dormant. The orchard still existed, but it was overgrown. Most of the trees were in bad shape. The weeds were as tall as me and I am five foot three. It was a huge project to start an urban garden there, so we had to raise money. We went to a family foundation and they ended up funding the start of the project. We broke ground there in April

2016. We just obtained a contract with the Los Angeles Unified School District, so we're an official vendor. We have the land for three years and the middle school is so excited.

Watts, Los Angeles is an area known as a food desert. There is no supermarket providing healthy food. It's also a neighborhood of gangs, drugs, and a high crime rate. When you go there and talk to the kids, their faces have hope. They know the difference between where they live compared to where other people live not very far from them. When we started cleaning the land and began working with the students there was an immediate shift. The school currently has 800 students to date. We talk about loving yourself, soil health, growing your own food, nutrition, and healing. They are beginning to take ownership. They are growing food that they had never eaten before. By the end of our first summer, the kids were eating kale and cucumbers. They were picking peppers. They were picking carrots out of the ground and eating them. It is so exciting to see their faces light up. We are now officially working with the Boys and Girls Club at the school and we have a three day a week garden club. We've also joined forces with other community agencies, including the Watts Gang Task Force and the Watts Neighborhood Council.

We are working on nutrition programs and bringing on partners for curriculum. Our goal is to create a working farm and have the students and community eat from it. We would like to create hundreds of pounds of food a week. We just put in a greenhouse at the middle school. We are raising money to create a model that we can take into other urban Los Angeles schools that have dormant pieces of land or a field that they used to use for sports. We can use that land to grow food and create a sustainable model. The food could be sold to local restaurants or elsewhere in the community. The food could be given away.

Who is someone you admire?

Alice Waters is someone I admire. She really started this movement with something called The Edible Schoolyard Project. We're going to hopefully get more involved and have something like her program here. This would include having curriculum that reaches into different subject areas.

Discover more about Community Healing Gardens at www.communityhealinggardens.org

Cliff Mayotte

Education Program Director, Voice of Witness
San Francisco, California

"Empathy takes courage and resilience."

Please tell me about the mission of Voice of Witness.

Voice of Witness seeks to use oral history as a foundation to illuminate stories of contemporary injustice. We wish to impact the way people share narrative and process stories of injustice from around the world. We hope to impact both the speaker and the listener. Part of our mission is to amplify stories of social justice and human rights issues that are either underreported or underrepresented and to create a platform or a megaphone for these stories to be heard. We hope to broaden people's perspectives and to complicate their thinking in a really useful way and to put a human face on contemporary social justice issues. We want to go beyond the statistic or the single story about a particular issue, a culture, a community, or an individual.

The Voice of Witness education program follows along those same principles and takes those ideas and brings them in the classroom. We look at using narrative and first person narrative to unpack social, cultural, and historical forces that are shaping these stories. We want to make space for students to not only grapple with these issues through a personal narrative, which sometimes can be a lot more meaningful and a lot more relevant to them, but also to share our methodology and our oral history practice so communities and classrooms can share their own stories and amplify their own unheard voices.

Our education program is also a professional development opportunity for educators. It is not only useful for learning how to conduct oral history projects, but the oral history process and the methodology behind it is useful and impactful. It creates a space for teachers to get to know their students and to create projects and work on things together as opposed to just making work for the students. It shifts the culture and the dynamics of a classroom both for students and teachers.

We are now broadening who we're working with in terms of that methodology. We are going beyond educators in the classroom and branching into healthcare and the legal profession. We are doing these kinds of consultancies with people who see the value in amplifying unheard voices, storytelling, active listening, and nurturing empathy.

Please tell me about a few projects that the education program has inspired.

One inspiring project occurred at Oakland Technical High School. We had been doing oral history work with some of their history classes and we also did a little bit with one of their theater classes. We taught students interview techniques, because they were doing small scale oral history-based performances. About 18 months ago, the theater teacher got in contact with me and said, "All of the students and myself were really inspired by the Voice of Witness book, *Voices from the Storm,*" which is a book of oral history focused around Hurricane Katrina. They were interested in working with us to develop a play version of the book.

We consulted with them over several months. The students are incredibly courageous, empathic, and curious. They dove into the process and created an 80-minute play version of *Voices from the Storm*, which was incredibly powerful. They were able to look at these stories of displacement and people who had been marginalized before, during, and after Hurricane Katrina, and connect with issues of income inequality and gentrification in their own communities.

Another project we just finished was a consultancy with the University of California, San Francisco, which is a very large medical research and teaching hospital. They have a Memory and Aging Center, which is devoted to the care, treatment, practice, and study of dementia, aging, and Alzheimer's. Last year, Voice of Witness was the artist-in-residence at the Memory and Aging Center and we embarked on this large-scale project in which we collected oral histories from patients, nurses, caregivers, doctors, and psychologists. We helped them create an oral history book called, *Hear/Say*, about the realities of dementia, Alzheimer's, and aging. It is incredibly powerful.

I believe what these projects and others have in common is empathy. People use the word empathy a lot. It's become very sexy. It's a buzzword. I think it tends to be something that people use as a feel-good phrase. People may say, "I empathize with you. I can connect with you. I identify with you." I think that's definitely a part of empathy, but I think empathy as a daily practice is hard. Empathy takes courage and resilience. Empathy is directly related to inquiry and an intense curiosity about the experiences of other people. Part of empathy is also a way to acknowledge difference. There is so much that connects us, but we need to have the courage to say that we're not all the same. People have wildly different experiences for so many different reasons, whether it's geography, language, socioeconomics, religion, racism, or many other things. Practicing empathy is a way to acknowledge these differences and that is where the activism comes in. It's not just to merely acknowledge, but to do something.

Who is someone you admire?

I tend to be drawn towards very courageous and outspoken artists that use their work, whether they are writers, painters, or filmmakers, to go past art for art's sake. They are connected to excellence in their craft, but they realize that there's a lot that needs to be talked about. James Baldwin is someone I admire who has these qualities. Studs Terkel is another. He was an incredible listener and very curious about other people. Anna Deavere Smith, a theater artist, is also a person who is inspiring for all of the above reasons. Folks that inspire me are other storytellers, because what I do is ultimately connected to narrative and storytelling.

Discover more about Voice of Witness, including the education program and book series, at voiceofwitness.org

Carolyn Merino Mullin

Co-founder and Executive Director, The Animal Museum
Los Angeles, California

"Truly, the museum brings me a lot of joy."

How did you become interested in animal rights?

Like a lot of kids, I had a natural affinity for animals and this innate need to help them. Mine has been a life-long trajectory of trying to do just that. To discover animal rights in middle school by way of PETA literature was probably inevitable. I then read whatever I could find on animal rights and what was happening. It was catastrophic. I started an animal rights club in high school. My passion for activism and organizing took off from there, and it's never stopped.

What is the mission of The Animal Museum?

Our main role has been to fill a long vacant niche in the museum field. Unlike every other social justice movement, whether civil rights, women's suffrage, or the labor movement, which have their own institutions preserving and sharing their histories and continuing their legacies, there was no animal protection museum anywhere. When people go to these museums, they have transformative experiences. That's the heart of what we're here to do: to be a home for animal protection, and to inspire current and future generations of animal lovers and advocates.

Tell me more about the museum's *My Dog is My Home* exhibit.

The curator of *My Dog is My Home* was a former intern of ours named Christine Kim. Back then she was a social worker on Skid Row here in downtown Los Angeles, and she witnessed firsthand that the homeless who have animal companions were falling through the cracks. They were being denied admission into places and thus being denied services, because they had an animal. They couldn't find housing that allowed animals, but most would not relinquish their animals, opting to stay on the streets. That is their family. For many of them, anecdotally, it's a reason to live. They are someone to love who loves them back.

We decided to do an exhibit based on this, and it really opened a lot of hearts and minds, including my own. I think I was the first to cast judgment. I thought, "If you can't take care of yourself, what makes you think you can take care of an animal?" That was shattered during this exhibit, which follows the lives of four homeless families over the course of a year. By the end of the exhibit, visitors learn that three out of the four families are off the streets, and they attribute that to having an animal. Their dogs gave them a reason to live and a reason to be responsible. They wanted to do better for their animal companions. It's just really incredible.

Christine, similar to me starting the museum, decided to take a leap of faith and establish her own non-profit. She's now consulting with cities across the country to help meet the needs of their homeless populations with animals and getting shelters to open up accompanying facilities for dogs and cats.

What do you do to stay motivated and how do you continue to have hope?

When I was first becoming an activist in my mid to late teens, I had a lot of anger. And naturally so. It's a long, hard road to extinguish animal cruelty, abuse, and neglect, and that's incredibly frustrating, but that mindset does no one any good. No one wants to hang out with an angry, outraged person. I've had this personal journey of finding my niche of activism. Truly, the museum brings me a lot of joy. I love connecting with people and visitors who come through our space. Activism can be really fun, rewarding, and fulfilling.

I noticed you recently had a group of college students tour the museum. Can you tell me about that experience?

The Animals and Society Institute is an amazing non-profit, and they encourage universities to start minors, majors, or even Ph.D. programs in animal studies, and now, apparently, student groups! The University of Redlands, which is over an hour away, happens to have one.

These students have been taking multidisciplinary courses that specialize in animals, like philosophy, conservation, and the like. For many animal lovers, it's an immediate draw when you go to the university and you see these classes. They decided to make this field trip as part of their club, and it was really encouraging. They're bright, young, and excited minds who want to do good in the world, and I know they will.

Tell me about someone you admire.

Her name is Caroline Earle White. She was born and raised in Philadelphia as a Quaker in the 1800s, and had an innate love for animals. In her era, she routinely witnessed carriage horses, overburdened with people or cargo, beaten mercilessly. A lot of times, they were abandoned in the streets when they were no longer of use, and it broke her heart, but fueled a fire within her. She refused to even take carriages, so she walked everywhere, and eventually started one of the early Society for the Prevention of Cruelty to Animals (SPCA) in the country: the Pennsylvania SPCA.

Because she was a woman, she wasn't allowed to be on the board of directors; her husband had to be her voice. As a vocal suffragette, she wouldn't stand for that and consequently established the Women's Branch of the Pennsylvania SPCA. During her time there, she received a request to relinquish the animals in her care to a laboratory and she was shocked that animals were being experimented on in the United States. What does this tenacious woman do? She started the American Anti-Vivisection Society, which was the first group to combat or take on animal testing.

Caroline was such a vivacious woman, and she cared about so many issues, including orphaned children and slavery. I just love that we are standing on the shoulders of individuals like her. I love her. I consider her the grandmother of animal protection.

Discover more about The Animal Museum and view online exhibits at www.theanimalmuseum.com

Lauren Ornelas

Founder and Executive Director, Food Empowerment Project
Cotati, California

"Our individual choices and our collective voices can make a difference."

Please share about your work with the Food Empowerment Project. What are the organization's different projects?

Food Empowerment Project is a vegan food justice organization. We work on promoting veganism for the animals and getting people to think about animals as sentient beings and to not consume them. We do this in a variety of ways. We have information on veganism and how animals are treated on our website. We also have a website called VeganMexicanFood. com. Both sites are available in English and Spanish.

We do monthly protests in front of the chicken slaughterhouse in our community. We want people who drive by to not ignore who is being killed inside. We also have whistleblower cards that we hand out to the workers at the slaughterhouse.

We have a newsletter to help people go and stay vegan. Right now we're in the research gathering phase, and we hope to re-launch it again later this year. Subscribers get one issue a month for a year. We created a print version, because we know not everybody has access to the Internet 24/7. We wanted to make it so that they could read it on the bus or wherever it is convenient for them.

We also act in solidarity with farm workers who pick our food. We do this by supporting corporate campaigns, including the boycott against

Wendy's and the boycott against Driscoll's Berries. We work in supporting good legislation for farm workers and opposing bad legislation for them. We're also working right now to change a regulation that impacts the education of the children of farm workers. We coordinate a school supply drive for the children of farm workers as well.

Another area of our work is around getting people to not buy chocolate sourced from the worst forms of child labor, including slavery. We contact over 100 companies a year and ask them where they source their chocolate from. From that we create a list of chocolates that we do and don't recommend. The list is updated monthly. We also have an app for Android and iPhones that people can download for free. To make our recommended list, a company has to make at least one vegan chocolate.

We also work on lack of access to healthy foods in communities of color and low-income communities. We research the availability of healthy produce and alternatives to "meat" and dairy. We make an assessment of the community and we share that with policy makers. Then we follow up and do focus groups within the community. We want people to be able to go vegan for the sake of the animals as well as for their health. We know that not everybody has access to healthy food. By doing this work we hope to increase the availability of these foods.

We currently have a campaign against Safeway. In doing our work on lack of access to healthy foods in Vallejo, California, we found that Safeway moved one of their grocery stores from a low-income community of color to a suburban area further away. When they left they put a restrictive deed on their former property preventing another grocery store from moving in for 15 years – effectively leaving that community without a grocery store. We found they have done this in other cities in the U.S. After communicating directly with one of their Vice Presidents for months, we decided to take this campaign to the public – which we started in October of 2016.

How did you learn about animal rights and become vegan?

I went vegetarian when I was really young. My mom told me what chicken was, and I decided I didn't want to be responsible for killing chickens, so I stopped eating them. In elementary school I was vegetarian. In between that time and when I turned 16, my family didn't have a lot of money, so I just ate what people gave us. I went back to consuming animals. By the time I was 16, I decided that I was going to eat peanut butter and jelly every day. I did not want to eat animals again.

It wasn't until I was 17 that I learned about animal rights. This was in 1987. I immediately got in touch with a local animal rights group. I had already stopped wearing leather, but I was still consuming dairy and eggs. After getting in touch with this group, I became an animal rights activist. It will be 30 years ago this year.

As an activist aware of so much suffering in the world, what do you do to take care of yourself and remain positive?

Every time I learn about various abuses, which seems to be on a regular basis, my first instinct is to figure out what I can do to stop contributing to it. My second instinct is to figure out how I can not only use my own choices to make a difference, but how I can join in with others to try and make a difference.

I've been doing this for 30 years now, and I haven't really gotten burnt out. I think some of the reason is because I am always willing to learn new things. I'm willing to change. When I first got involved, I focused primarily on anti-vivisection. Then I did anti-captivity campaigns. That followed with a focus on factory farming and veganism issues. I've been doing that for 17 or 18 years now, but I still changed. I did investigations of factory farms and slaughterhouses. I did corporate campaigns. Now I'm still promoting veganism, but I'm doing it in a different way. I'm reaching out to different communities. I think that all of that helps me from getting burnt out.

Who are others you admire?

There are so many. I admire Dolores Huerta. She co-founded the United Farm Workers. I also admire Steve Biko who was an anti-apartheid activist. And I admire Henry David Thoreau.

Is there anything else you would like to share with others?

I understand how things can be overwhelming for people. Let's say you just learned about veganism and you're overwhelmed. You decide you're going to become vegan. Then you learn about the chocolate issue and so on. I always encourage people to not be overwhelmed, but instead look at these as opportunities to make a difference. Our individual choices and our collective voices can make a difference. People can start by eating their ethics, and making sure that everything they put in their mouths is something they actually support.

There's a lot of suffering going on in this world. I think that's one of the reasons why Food Empowerment Project chose to focus on food. We eat several times a day. With our food choices we can do something consistently. We have a greater responsibility to be informed consumers and make sure that we are eating our ethics.

Discover more about Food Empowerment Project at www.foodispower.org and veganmexicanfood.com

Kim Sherobbi

Director, Birwood House and Board Member, James and Grace Lee Boggs
Center to Nurture Community Leadership
Detroit, Michigan

"It is important to be able to use your imagination to create the kind of
community, neighborhood, and family that you want and to take on that
responsibility."

Please tell me about the mission of the Birwood House and some of
the projects you have been involved with.

The mission of the Birwood House is to nurture community leadership by
getting people engaged and taking an active part in their community. We
want people to understand that they have the power and responsibility to
create the kind of community they want.

I am a lifelong resident of Birwood Street. I've lived here for over
50 years. My neighborhood work is derived from my childhood experiences. My mother and her peers provided a safe and nurturing place for me
and all the other children who lived on the block. I wish people of all ages
could experience the loving and caring relationships, between neighbors, I
experienced when I was growing up.

Presently, I'm involved in a project called Community Lens, which
is a community engagement project for middle school students who attend
Noble School. Program participants will use cameras as their tool to learn
about the challenges and opportunities in their neighborhoods. At the
end of the program, students will attend a regional community forum

sponsored by Semis, which is an initiative housed at Eastern Michigan University. Students will submit a photo accompanied by a written description. At the forum, Noble students will get to present their photo. They will also be able to hear other students in the region share their projects.

In addition to interacting with students from Noble School, this summer I will have a chance to work with high school students in the Youth Energy Squad (YES) program. The YES program focuses on green sustainability and community engagement. During a Birwood Block Club Association meeting, YES Members will have a conversation with Birwood residents to find out how they can help us with our green infrastructure. Most of the block club members are elders, so I'm excited about the intergenerational dialogue and the potential for older and younger people to work together. The high school students will bring more energy and new ideas to Birwood Street. Hopefully, lifelong relationships will develop and a sense of community power will be reinforced.

When you asked me about my involvement with community projects, it caused me to think of how often people want to see immediate tangible results without being concerned about the sustainability of the project. It's important for community projects to last, because people frequently get depressed when they don't see their efforts valued. Therefore, it's essential to spend time creating a caring, conscious, and educated community. The work of community building is not always concrete and usually has no time limit. One never really knows how long it will take for a significant number of people in a community to do the internal work to sustain it. That's really the focus of the Birwood House: to support and nurture people in their personal development so our neighborhoods can thrive.

I'm a prime example of the internal work process. Being a member of the James and Grace Lee Boggs Center for about 15 years has afforded the insights and support needed for me to develop myself enough to provide the similar support to people in my neighborhood. Transformation of one's self is a journey to be cherished not a product to be counted or compared.

Because you've lived on Birwood Street for so long, can you tell me a little about the history of the street?

My parents purchased their home on Birwood Street in 1958. They were the first black family to purchase a home in the neighborhood. They integrated the block. Therefore, I experienced the changing of the block from stable middle class families to about 40% renters. Some houses on Birwood Street are now dilapidated and burned-down. The conditions of the houses are partly due to racism, unethical practices of some banks, governmental officials, and corporations. I remember when the 1967 Rebellion happened. I was about eight years old. I remember feeling scared hearing the fire engines and loud noises, because I did not know what was going on. I also sensed the panic in my mother and watched the chaos on television. After learning about the history of the rebellion, I can now identify with many of the circumstances that caused the 1967 Rebellion and my fears at the time. Today, my community faces some of the same social dynamics that were present then.

Even with the numerous challenges people in my neighborhood confront, there is still a foundation of community spirit to build on. Some people, like myself, decided to stay and take responsibility for maintaining and building our area. We're not stuck here. We've chosen to stay in our neighborhood. Blending the different kinds of lifestyles is not always easy to manage but we are learning how to do it in a non-violent and productive manner. Hopefully, we are becoming more mature and wiser people in the process. Living on Birwood Street has enabled me to fully understand what it means to be a member of a neighborhood community.

Can you tell me about someone you admire?

There are so many people that I admire. My mother was my hero. She died in 1994. However, one of the people I admire is Raziya Curtis. Raziya is co-founder of Healing Support Network. She is committed to assisting people heal through traditional and alternative methods. Raziya has operated the Network for over 20 years. I have witnessed the transformation of many people whose lives she's influenced. Raziya welcomes people from all walks of life to improve their mind, body, and spirit. She has such a loving way about herself.

I want to also emphasize how much the Boggs Center has meant to my personal development and how grateful I am for having found the organization. During these challenging times in America, people are waking up from the American Dream and are realizing that America is something other than the dream it offered. Being a member of the Boggs Center has enabled me to keep life in perspective and stay empowered.

Discover more about the James and Grace Lee Boggs Center to Nurture Community Leadership at boggscenter.org

Love Activism Practices

This is a complete list of all the practices mentioned at the ends of earlier chapters. If you find it inspiring, consider photocopying or scanning/ printing these pages and hanging them up where you will often see them.

Practices of Service: cook a meal for your friend or partner; visit the ill; take someone to a medical appointment; clean or make repairs for someone; provide literacy tutoring; bring food to the poor and their companion animals; mail books to prisoners; volunteer to clean litter at the ocean or other natural area; mail someone a surprise postcard; walk dogs at a shelter or for elderly or disabled neighbors with limited mobility; start a community reading group; be an advocate for foster youth; call or visit someone who may be lonely; adopt an old animal; grow plants that help the environment thrive; visit cats at a shelter…

Practices of Empathy: listen deeply to someone's story; read memoirs and oral histories of individuals with experiences both similar and different from you; do not judge another's suffering; think kind thoughts or pray for those in need; boycott circuses or places that use animals for entertainment; volunteer to answer calls on a suicide hotline; study and read about racism and other forms of injustice; meditate on how you would feel in another's difficult situation; look into self-help practices to maintain your balance and wellbeing…

Practices of Hope: smile at strangers; plant a tree; join a community garden or start gardening at home; start reading a great, big book; enroll in a class you always wanted to take; reflect on the positive outcome of a loving act you performed; make a gratitude or future possibilities list you can refer to daily; create an altar or peaceful place; list future inspiring events on a calendar; create a vision board...

Practices of Non-Violence: go vegan; reject racist jokes; buy fair trade clothing, coffee, and other goods; boycott companies that profit from violence; stand up to bullies; speak out against war; buy organic food; buy cruelty free cosmetics and cleaning supplies; capture and release insects...

Practices of Self-Care: talk with a therapist or spiritual advisor; rest when you are tired; ride a bike; take walks; love and accept your body; forgive yourself, remembering that we all make mistakes; ask for help/tell a friend when you are suffering; take a bubble bath; find body-positive resources; reject media that does not heal and nourish your soul...

Practices of Creativity: teach someone how to paint or play an instrument; write poetry; collage; make handmade cards for your friends; visit a museum; see an independent film; donate to an art organization; take an art class; cook/bake; support local artists; send a "thank you" note to a writer, poet, or artist you admire; read about self-taught artists; support community radio stations that feature local artists; create a zine...

Practices of Feminism: reject sexist jokes; do not critique women's bodies; study women's history and feminism; support feminist presses and bookstores; read memoirs and autobiographies of women from diverse cultures and economic backgrounds; speak out against violence against women; donate clothing or other goods to a domestic violence shelter; create or join a feminist consciousness-raising group; read and research to become aware of global crimes against women...

Practices of Mindfulness: be deeply present for someone; eat some silent meals; turn off the television/get rid of your television; meditate; eat slowly; offer kind and authentic self-expression; offer/practice deep listening; have moments of silence in your life; refrain from major decisions when you are confused...

Recommended Reading And Listening For Love Activists

The following resources, several of which were mentioned throughout *Love Activism*, are recommended for continued growth, study, and inspiration.

Adams, Carol J. *The Sexual Politics of Meat: A Feminist-Vegetarian Critical Theory*. New York, NY: Bloomsbury, 1990.

Adichie, Chimamanda Ngozi. *We Should All Be Feminists*. New York, NY: Anchor Books, 2015.

Allen, Pat B. *Art is a Spiritual Path: Engaging the Sacred through the Practice of Art and Writing*. Boston, MA: Shambhala, 2005.

Allen, Pat B. *Art is a Way of Knowing: A Guide to Self-Knowledge and Spiritual Fulfillment through Creativity*. Boston, MA: Shambhala, 1995.

Bayles, David, and Ted Orland. *Art & Fear: Observations on the Perils (and Rewards) of Artmaking*. Santa Cruz, CA: Image Continuum, 1993.

Butler, C. T., and Keith McHenry. *Food Not Bombs*. Tucson, AZ: See Sharp Press, 2000.

Chapman, Mare. *Unshakeable Confidence: The Freedom to Be Our Authentic Selves*. Madison, WI: Mare Chapman, LLC, 2017.

Corbett, Sarah. *A Little Book of Craftivism*. London, England: Cicada Books, 2013.

Davis, Angela Y. *Women, Race, & Class*. New York, NY: Random House, 1981.

Davis, Brenda, and Vesanto Melina. *Becoming Vegan: The Complete Reference to Plant-Based Nutrition*. Summertown, TN: Book Publishing Company, 2014.

Diamond, Irene, and Gloria Orenstein. *Reweaving the World: The Emergence of Ecofeminism*. San Francisco, CA: Sierra Club Books, 1990.

Estes, Clarissa Pinkola. *The Joyous Body: Myths & Stories of the Wise Woman Archetype.* Boulder, CO: Sounds True, 2011. CD.

Estes, Clarissa Pinkola. *Theatre of the Imagination: A Treasure of Healing Stories.* Boulder, CO: Sounds Trues, 1995. CD.

Estes, Clarissa Pinkola. *Women Who Run with the Wolves.* New York, NY: Ballantine Books, 1992.

Gay, Roxane. *Hunger: A Memoir of (My) Body.* New York, NY: HarperCollins, 2017.

Greer, Betsy. *Craftivism: The Art of Craft and Activism.* Vancouver, British Columbia: Arsenal Pulp Press, 2014.

Hanh, Thich Nhat. *At Home in the World.* Berkeley, CA: Parallax Press, 2016.

Hanh, Thich Nhat. *How to Eat.* Berkeley, CA: Parallax Press, 2014.

Hanh, Thich Nhat. *How to Love.* Berkeley, CA: Parallax Press, 2015.

Harper, A. Breeze. *Sistah Vegan: Black Female Vegans Speak on Food, Identity, Health, and Society.* New York, NY: Lantern Book, 2010.

Holmes, Seth. *Fresh Fruit, Broken Bodies: Migrant Farmworkers in the United States.* Berkeley, California: University of California Press, 2013.

hooks, bell. *All About Love: New Visions.* New York, NY: Harper Perennial, 2000.

hooks, bell. *Communion: The Female Search for Love.* New York, NY: HarperCollins, 2002.

hooks, bell. *Feminism is for Everybody.* Cambridge, MA: South End Press, 2000.

Jordan, June. *Life as Activism: June Jordan's Writings from the Progressive,* edited by Stacy Russo. Sacramento, CA: Litwin Books, 2014.

McNiff, Shaun. *Art Heals: How Creativity Cures the Soul.* Boulder, CO: Shambhala, 2004.

Mike, and Isy. *Another Dinner is Possible: More Than Just a Vegan Cookbook.* Oakland, CA: AK Press, 2009.

Moore, Thomas. *The Re-Enchantment of Everyday Life.* New York, NY: HarperCollins, 1996.

Moskowitz, Isa Chandra. *Vegan with a Vengeance: Over 150 Delicious, Cheap, Animal-Free Recipes That Rock.* New York, NY: Marlowe & Company, 2005.

Neruda, Pablo. *Odes to Common Things.* New York, NY: Bulfinch Press, 1994.

Oldenburg, Ray. *The Great Good Place: Cafes, Coffee Shops, Bookstores, Bars, Hair Salons and Other Hangouts at the Heart of a Community.* New York, NY: Marlowe & Company, 1989.

Oliveros, Pauline. *Deep Listening: A Composer's Sound Practice.* New York, NY: iUniverse, 2005.

Piercy, Marge. *My Life, My Body.* Oakland, CA: PM Press, 2015.

Queen Afua. *Sacred Woman: A Guide to Healing the Feminine Body, Mind, and Spirit.* New York, NY: Random House, 2000.

Shiva, Vandana. *Earth Democracy: Justice, Sustainability, and Peace.* Berkeley, CA: North Atlantic Books, 2005.

Solnit, Rebecca. *Men Explain Things to Me.* Chicago, IL: Haymarket Books, 2014.

Solnit, Rebecca. *The Mother of All Questions.* Chicago, IL: Haymarket Books, 2017.

Starhawk. *The Earth Path: Grounding Your Spirit in the Rhythms of Nature.* New York, NY: HarperCollins, 2005.

Tea, Michelle, ed. *Without a Net: The Female Experience of Growing Up Working Class*. Emeryville, CA: Seal Press, 2003.

Terkel, Studs. *Working: People Talk about What They Do All Day and How They Feel about What They Do*. New York, NY: The New Press, 2004.

Books from the Voice of Witness oral history series, including:

Eggers, Dave. *The Voice of Witness Reader: Ten Years of Amplifying Unheard Voices*. San Francisco, CA: McSweeney's Books, 2015.

Orner, Peter, and Luis Urrea. *Underground America: Narratives of Undocumented Lives*. London, England: Verso, 2008.

Vollen, Lola, and Dave Eggers. *Surviving Justice: America's Wrongfully Convicted and Exonerated*. San Francisco, CA: McSweeney's Books, 2008.

Questions for Self-Reflection and Reading Groups

1. Do you call yourself an activist? Why or why not?

2. Do you agree with the author that Love Activism should include all living beings?

3. The Living Portraits: Interviews With Activists section presented people and organizations that illustrate the elements discussed in this book. If you were to add a living portrait, who would it be?

4. Can you think of a profound time when you received Love Activism from another person in the form of service or empathy? How did this make you feel?

5. Creativity is defined as one of the Eight Beautiful Elements of Love Activism. What does creativity look like in your life?

6. Do you feel a connection to the environment and natural world?

7. In the section on Mindfulness, there is a discussion on cultivating silence and quiet in our lives. Do you currently have silence and quiet in your life? If not, do you see value in cultivating them?

8. What practices of self-care do you have in your life?

9. Do you call yourself a feminist? Why or why not?

10. Veganism is presented in the book as a practice of Love Activism tied to the element of non-violence. If you currently eat animals, has reading this book made you question this?

11. In the section on Hope, there is a mention of creating vision boards as a hopeful practice. If you were to make a vision board today, what would your intention be?

12. Have you had any experiences caring for an older or ailing animal? Did this experience transform you in any way?

13. In Renee Folzenlogen's interview she mentions returning to school later in life and becoming a licensed art therapist at age 54. If you are in your middle or later years, is there something you would like to embark on that would impact your work toward a better world? What can you do to begin putting this goal in action?

14. In Cliff Mayotte's interview he comments, "Empathy takes courage and resilience. Empathy is directly related to inquiry and an intense curiosity about the experiences of other people. Part of empathy is also a way to acknowledge difference." Does this make you feel different about the word empathy within an activist context?

15. Kim Sherobbi discusses living on Birwood Street in Detroit for over 50 years in her interview, which has allowed her to see changes in her neighborhood and build a strong personal connection with her community. How long have you lived in your neighborhood? Do you consider your neighborhood a community? If not, what ways could you contribute to building community?

16. Kim Sherobbi states, "Transformation of one's self is a journey to be cherished – not a product to be counted or compared." This is different from a culture that often wants to assign value based on tangible evidence, such as statistics and quantitative results. Does her description of what she calls the "internal work process" resonate with you? Why or why not?

17. Do you agree that hearing and listening are not the same? How is listening a part of your activism?

18. Nicholas Kristof's article with the provocative title, "Husbands Are Deadlier than Terrorists," was mentioned in the Feminism chapter. Does this statement make you think differently about feminism and male violence? Do you agree with Kristof's (or the editor's) decision for the article's title?

19. Are you able to practice service in your work?

20. Did reading this book make you want to change anything about your life?

With Gratitude

Thankful for my amazing brother David and his wife Linda. Thankful for the support, love, and companionship of Steven Soto. Thankful for all of the experiences and talks with Renie Felipe. Thankful for the beautiful soul of Annie Knight in many ways. Thankful for the support of my friend Nina Clements. Thankful for Laura Beth Bachman's enthusiasm and support. Thankful for my wild writing companions Joni and Mr. Pipps. Thankful for Victoria's wisdom. Thankful for California, coffee, chocolate, and the ocean. Thankful for the students of Santa Ana College. Thankful for my professors at Cypress College, UC Berkeley, Chapman University, and San Jose State University and for all the gifts they gave me. Thankful for Rory Litwin and Litwin Books for believing in this book and my previous book on June Jordan. And always thankful for my parents, Rena and Dave Shotsberger – you are greatly missed.

About the Author

Stacy Russo, a librarian and professor at Santa Ana College in Santa Ana, California, is a writer, poet, and artist. Her previous books are *We Were Going to Change the World: Interviews with Women from the 1970s/1980s Southern California Punk Rock Scene* (Santa Monica Press); *Life as Activism: June Jordan's Writings from The Progressive* (Litwin Books); and *The Library as Place in California* (McFarland). Her articles, poetry, and reviews have appeared in *Feminist Teacher, Feminist Collections, American Libraries, Counterpoise, Library Journal, Chaffey Review, Serials Review,* and the anthology *Open Doors: An Invitation to Poetry* (Chaparral Canyon Press). She holds degrees from the University of California, Berkeley; Chapman University; and San Jose State University.

Visit www.love-activism.com or www.facebook.com/loveactivism to join the global Love Activism Community.

Send email to stacy@love-activism.com to reach Stacy directly.

Index

CPSIA information can be obtained
at www.ICGtesting.com
Printed in the USA
FSHW02n0430130618
49094FS

9 781634 000550